Math
Skills

Grade 6

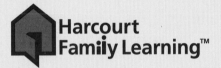
Harcourt Family Learning™

FLASH KIDS and the distinctive Flash Kids logo are registered trademarks of Barnes & Noble Booksellers, Inc.
Harcourt Family Learning and Design is a trademark of Harcourt, Inc.

© 2004 Flash Kids
Adapted from *Steck-Vaughn Working with Numbers. Level F*
© 2001 Harcourt Achieve
Licensed under special arrangement with Harcourt Achieve.

For more information, please visit flashkids.com
Please submit all inquiries to Flashkids@sterlingpublishing.com

ISBN 978-1-4114-0111-2

Manufactured in China

Lot #:
34 36 38 40 39 37 35
04/19

Illustrator: Lauren Scheuer

FlashKids
New York

Dear Parent,

As you bring math learning into the home, you are helping your child to strengthen the skills that he or she is taught in the classroom. Your efforts also emphasize how math is useful outside of school, as well as necessary for success in everyday life.

To assist you, this colorful, fun workbook presents grade-appropriate math concepts and language to your child in a way that is logical and organized. Each section begins with clear examples that illustrate new skills, and then practice drills, problem-solving lessons, and unit reviews encourage your child to master each new technique.

This Grade 6–level workbook begins by exercising your child's competence with addition, subtraction, multiplication, and division techniques. Units 2 and 3 fully develop skills with fractions, teaching sophisticated addition and subtraction problems as well as introducing multiplication and division of simple and complex fractions. Next, Units 4 and 5 demonstrate fraction and decimal equivalents, and then methods to solve problems containing decimal forms. Units 6 reviews your child's grasp of customary and metric units of measure, and lastly Unit 7 introduces the use of formulas for calculating area, perimeter, and volume.

As you and your child work through each unit, try to show your child how to apply each skill in everyday situations. For example, each time that you add bags of individually priced produce items to your grocery cart, you can ask your child to calculate the new total, including the added tax, to help you ensure that the bill will not go over the shopping budget. This exercise requires your child to apply many different math skills to a single, real-life problem. As your child draws connections between concepts presented separately in this workbook, he or she learns to reason mathematically, an ability critical for success through future years of math instruction.

Also, consider how you can turn the following activities into fun math exercises for you and your child to do together:

- Comparing marked distances between towns and other sites during car trips;

- Purchasing enough food and drinks for a family dinner or a party;

- Estimating the proper tip for a restaurant bill;

- Calculating how much material is needed to make new curtains, build bookshelves, or carpet a room;

- Devising a plan to save money for a special purchase;

- Measuring ingredients to be used in cooking, and if necessary, dividing amounts to adjust the recipe.

Use your imagination! With help from you and this workbook, your child is well on the way to math proficiency.

Table of Contents

unit 1

Whole Numbers and Operations

unit 2

Fractions

unit 3

Multiplication and Division of Fractions

unit 1
whole numbers and operations

Place Value

A **place-value chart** can help you understand **whole numbers**. Each **digit** in a number has a value based on its place in the number.

The digit 6 means 6 ten thousands, or 60,000.
The digit 2 means 2 thousands, or 2,000.
The digit 0 means 0 hundreds, or 0.
The digit 4 means 4 tens, or 40.
The digit 0 means 0 ones, or 0.

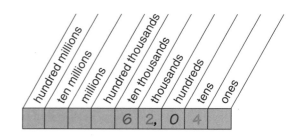

We read the number as sixty-two thousand, forty. Notice that commas are used to separate the digits into groups of three, called *periods*. This helps make larger numbers easier to read.

Write each number in the place-value chart.

1. 468,937,574

2. 5,910,382,654

3. 8,342,384

4. 76,098

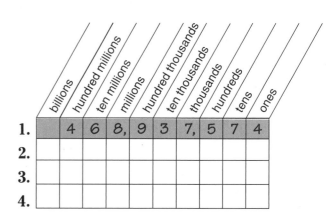

Write the place name for the digit 3 in each number.

	a		b
5. 56,837,784	ten thousands	887,654,321	
6. 90,543		675,345,242	
7. 898,865,436		3,876,544,098	
8. 3,565		24,356,540,912	

Write each number in words. Insert commas where needed.

9. 132,342 _____ one hundred thirty-two thousand, three hundred forty-two _____

10. 7,642,353_____

Comparing and Ordering Numbers

To compare two numbers, begin with the highest place value.
Compare the digits in each place.

The symbol < means **is less than**.　　　**23 < 57**
The symbol > means **is greater than**.　　**3 > 1**
The symbol = means **is equal to**.　　　**234 = 234**

Compare 354 and 57.

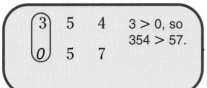

3 > 0, so
354 > 57.

Compare 2,243 and 1,542.

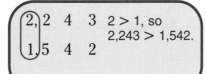

2 > 1, so
2,243 > 1,542.

Compare 134 and 187.

| 1 | 3 | 4 | The hundreds digits are the same. Compare the tens digits. |
| 1 | 8 | 7 | |

3 < 8, so 134 < 187.

Compare. Write <, >, or =.

　　　　　　　　a　　　　　　　　　　　　　　　　　　　*b*

1. 45 ___<___ 67　　　　　　　　　165 _____ 85

2. 23 _____ 57　　　　　　　　　34 _____ 598

3. 675 _____ 765　　　　　　　　654 _____ 654

4. 4,554 _____ 6,368　　　　　　4,342 _____ 4,367

5. 653 _____ 785　　　　　　　　4,321 _____ 824

6. 65,342 _____ 85,542　　　　　4,575 _____ 39,864

7. 973,765 _____ 1,000,000　　　453,643 _____ 255,764

Write in order from least to greatest.

8. 54　96　21 _____ *21　54　96* _____

9. 468　532　487 _____

10. 322　231　632 _____

11. 94,234　45,875　67,956 _____

12. 765,645　543,865　565,978 _____

13. 16,576　13,764　432,877 _____

Addition of Whole Numbers

To add, start with the digits in the ones place. Regroup as needed.

Find: 322 + 699

Add the ones. Regroup.	Add the tens.	Add the hundreds.

Th	H	T	O
		1	
	3	2	**2**
+	6	9	**9**
			1

Th	H	T	O
	1	1	
	3	**2**	2
+	6	**9**	9
		2	1

Th	H	T	O
1	1	1	
	3	2	2
+	**6**	9	9
1,	0	2	1

Add.

	a	b	c	d

1.

a)
Th	H	T	O
1	1	1	
	4	5	2
+	5	5	9
1,	0	1	1

b)
Th	H	T	O
	6	4	4
+	4	8	4

c)
Th	H	T	O
	5	1	7
+	5	6	3

d)
Th	H	T	O
	2	0	9
+	9	5	0

2.

a)
$$5,347$$
$$+9,520$$

b)
$$15,042$$
$$+86,996$$

c)
$$34,853$$
$$+47,532$$

d)
$$547,084$$
$$+743,754$$

3.

a)
$$342,535$$
$$+757,643$$

b)
$$74,574$$
$$+93,743$$

c)
$$355,684$$
$$+895,445$$

d)
$$546,783$$
$$+356,537$$

Line up the digits. Then find the sums.

	a	b

4. 6,535 + 5,764 = _____   543 + 528 = _____

$$6,535$$
$$+5,764$$

5. 231,456 + 76,421 = _____   341 + 4,352 = _____

Addition of Three or More Numbers

To add three or more numbers, use the same steps as when adding two numbers. Regroup as needed.

Find: 36 + 358 + 296

Add the ones. Regroup.	Add the tens.	Add the hundreds.

H	T	O
	2	
	3	6
3	5	8
+2	9	6
		0

H	T	O
1	2	
	3	6
3	5	8
+2	9	6
	9	0

H	T	O
1	2	
	3	6
3	5	8
+2	9	6
6	9	0

Add.

	a	b	c	d

1.

a:
Th	H	T	O
1	1	1	
	4	2	7
		7	8
+		8	4	3
1,	3	4	8

b:
Th	H	T	O
		2	0
	6	5	9
+	9	3	2

c:
Th	H	T	O
			7
	6	4	3
+		6	7

d:
Th	H	T	O
	3	2	5
	8	9	6
+			4

2.

a:
```
    3 9
  3 4 2
+ 6 9 0
```

b:
```
  4 7 9
  7 5 6
+   5 7
```

c:
```
    8 7 9
  3,9 5 0
+     4 3
```

d:
```
  3,4 0 4
    8 6 5
+ 7,4 3 6
```

3.

a:
```
  9 3 9,8 4 2
  8 7 4,8 9 0
    4 5,3 7 6
+ 4 3 2,9 8 6
```

b:
```
  6 3,9 2 8
  3 2,7 4 0
    5,3 2 1
+ 6 0,4 5 3
```

c:
```
  8 4 9,9 0 4
  4 3 2,8 4 0
  5 0 8,3 4 6
+ 5 6 7,7 8 5
```

d:
```
  5 8 9,4 9 3
  7 4 3,9 0 7
  9 0 8,3 5 4
+ 5 6 7,8 6 9
```

Line up the digits. Then find the sums.

	a		b

4. 554 + 860 + 64 = _____

```
  554
  860
+  64
```

379 + 940 + 390 = _____

Subtraction of Whole Numbers

To subtract, start with the digits in the ones place.
Regroup as needed.

Find: 715 − 239

Regroup. Subtract the ones.	Regroup. Subtract the tens.	Subtract the hundreds.

Regroup. Subtract the ones.

H	T	O
	0	15
7	1	5
−2	3	9
		6

Regroup. Subtract the tens.

H	T	O
6	10	15
7	1	5
−2	3	9
	7	6

Subtract the hundreds.

H	T	O
6	10	15
7	1	5
−2	3	9
4	7	6

Subtract.

	a	b	c	d
1.	$\begin{array}{c|c|c} H & T & O \\ & 11 & \\ 7 & 1 & 17 \\ 8 & 2 & 7 \\ -5 & 3 & 8 \\ \hline 2 & 8 & 9 \end{array}$	$\begin{array}{c|c|c} H & T & O \\ 7 & 4 & 2 \\ -5 & 4 & 4 \\ \hline & & \end{array}$	$\begin{array}{c|c|c} H & T & O \\ 1 & 3 & 5 \\ -1 & 2 & 9 \\ \hline & & \end{array}$	$\begin{array}{c|c|c} H & T & O \\ 6 & 5 & 6 \\ -5 & 0 & 7 \\ \hline & & \end{array}$
2.	$\begin{array}{r} 543 \\ -189 \\ \hline \end{array}$	$\begin{array}{r} 700 \\ -546 \\ \hline \end{array}$	$\begin{array}{r} 5,000 \\ -\ \ 899 \\ \hline \end{array}$	$\begin{array}{r} 7,643 \\ -4,908 \\ \hline \end{array}$
3.	$\begin{array}{r} 5,764 \\ -\ \ \ 200 \\ \hline \end{array}$	$\begin{array}{r} 43,675 \\ -23,507 \\ \hline \end{array}$	$\begin{array}{r} 439,709 \\ -234,564 \\ \hline \end{array}$	$\begin{array}{r} 742,457 \\ -\ 65,345 \\ \hline \end{array}$

Line up the digits. Then find the differences.

	a	b
4.	543 − 32 = _____	726 − 549 = _____
	$\begin{array}{r} 543 \\ -\ 32 \\ \hline \end{array}$	
5.	34,565 − 23,597 = _____	9,000 − 6,533 = _____

Estimation of Sums and Differences

To estimate a sum or difference, first round each number to the same place value. Then add or subtract the rounded numbers.

Estimate: 56,493 + 255

Round each number to the same place value. Add.

$$5\ 6,4\ 9\ 3 \rightarrow 56,500$$
$$+\ \ \ \ \ 2\ 5\ 5 \rightarrow +\ \ \ \ 300$$
$$56,800$$

Each number is rounded to the hundreds place.

Estimate: 39,465 − 442

Round each number to the same place value. Subtract.

$$3\ 9,4\ 6\ 5 \rightarrow 39,500$$
$$-\ \ \ \ \ 4\ 4\ 2 \rightarrow -\ \ \ 400$$
$$39,100$$

Each number is rounded to the hundreds place.

Estimate the sums.

	a	b	c	d
1.	$516 \rightarrow 500$ $+6,724 \rightarrow +6,700$	$4,332 \rightarrow$ $+\ \ 789 \rightarrow$	$53,500 \rightarrow$ $+\ \ \ \ 284 \rightarrow$	$4,325 \rightarrow$ $+534,643 \rightarrow$
2.	$8,583 \rightarrow$ $+2,393 \rightarrow$	$4,325 \rightarrow$ $+7,543 \rightarrow$	$6,436 \rightarrow$ $+8,964 \rightarrow$	$8,975 \rightarrow$ $+9,633 \rightarrow$

Estimate the differences.

	a	b	c	d
3.	$563 \rightarrow 600$ $-265 \rightarrow -300$	$895 \rightarrow$ $-435 \rightarrow$	$865 \rightarrow$ $-657 \rightarrow$	$975 \rightarrow$ $-864 \rightarrow$
4.	$53,864 \rightarrow$ $-\ \ \ 896 \rightarrow$	$14,535 \rightarrow$ $-2,356 \rightarrow$	$74,543 \rightarrow$ $-4,864 \rightarrow$	$49,564 \rightarrow$ $-7,534 \rightarrow$

Problem-Solving Method: Guess and Check

Thomas Jefferson was the sixth youngest person to sign the Declaration of Independence in 1776. Benjamin Franklin was 37 years older than Jefferson. The sum of their ages was 103. How old was Jefferson when he signed the Declaration of Independence?

Understand the problem.

- **What do you want to know?**
  Jefferson's age when he signed the Declaration of Independence

- **What information is given?**
  Clue 1: Jefferson's age + 37 = Franklin's age
  Clue 2: Jefferson's age + Franklin's age = 103

Plan how to solve it.

- **What method can you use?**
  You can guess an answer that satisfies the first clue.
  Then check to see if your answer satisfies the second clue.

Solve it.

- **How can you use this method to solve the problem?**
  Try to guess in an organized way so that each of your guesses gets closer to the exact answer. Use a table.

Guess Jefferson's Age	Check		Evaluate the Guess
	Clue 1	Clue 2	
30	30+37=67	30+67=97	too low
40	40+37=77	40+77=117	too high
35	35+37=72	35+72=107	too high
34	34+37=71	34+71=105	too high
33	33+37=70	33+70=103	satisfies both clues

- **What is the answer?**
  Thomas Jefferson was 33 years old when he signed the Declaration of Independence.

Look back and check your answer.

- **Is your answer reasonable?**
  You can check addition with subtraction.
  70 − 37 = 33
  103 − 70 = 33

  The addition checks and the age satisfies both clues.
  The answer is reasonable.

Use guess and check to solve each problem.

1. Aaron is 1 year younger than Laura. The sum of their ages is 23 years. How old is each of them?

Answer _____

2. Combined, the movies *Titanic* and *Gone with the Wind* won 19 Academy Awards. *Titanic* won 3 more awards than *Gone with the Wind.* How many awards did each movie win?

Answer _____

3. A millipede has 14 more legs than a caterpillar. Together they have 46 legs. How many legs does a caterpillar have?

Answer _____

4. Nicole did an aerobics class and a yoga class for a total of 1 hour and 10 minutes. The yoga class was 30 minutes longer than the aerobics class. How long was each class?

Answer _____

5. Alan has seven United States coins. Their total value is 61 cents. What coins and how many of each does he have?

Answer _____

Multiplication of One-digit and Two-digit Numbers

To multiply by one-digit numbers, use basic multiplication facts.
To multiply by two-digit numbers, multiply by the ones first. Then multiply by the tens.
Then add these two **partial products**.

Find: 38 × 42

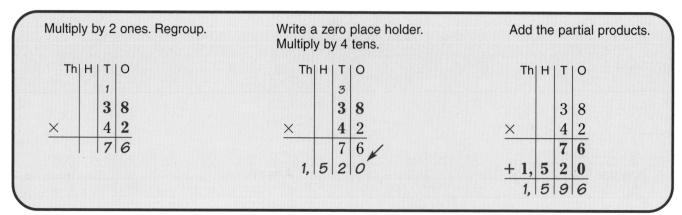

Multiply.

	a	b	c	d
1.	H T O 3 4 4 5 × 8 3 6 0	H T O 1 3 × 3	H T O 2 4 × 9	H T O 3 5 × 5
2.	1 4 5 × 6	6 0 1 × 3	7 6 4 × 7	9 4 2 × 8
3.	5 6 7 × 3 4	3 2 0 × 7 5	8 1 6 × 3 9	9 2 6 × 4 5
4.	1, 5 4 3 × 5 3	2, 6 5 0 × 9 7	2, 5 0 1 × 2 8	3 4, 6 0 3 × 3 5

Line up the digits. Then find the products.

a	b	c
5. 573 × 3 = _____	2,506 × 94 = _____	20,463 × 83 = _____

573
×   3

Zeros in Multiplication

When you multiply by tens, you need to write a zero as a **place holder**.

Remember,

- the product of 0 and any number is 0.
- the sum of 0 and any number is that number.

Find: 30 × 58

	Multiply by 0 ones.	Write a zero place holder. Multiply by 3 tens. Regroup.	Add the partial products.

Multiply by 0 ones.

```
Th| H | T | O
   |   | 5 | 8
 × |   | 3 | 0
   |   | 0 | 0
```

Write a zero place holder. Multiply by 3 tens. Regroup.

```
Th| H | T | O
   |   | 2 |
   |   | 5 | 8
 × |   | 3 | 0
   |   | 0 | 0        zero place
 1,| 7 | 4 | 0  ←     holder
```

Add the partial products.

```
Th| H | T | O
   |   | 5 | 8
 × |   | 3 | 0
   |   | 0 | 0
+1,| 7 | 4 | 0
 1,| 7 | 4 | 0
```

Multiply.

	a	*b*	*c*	*d*
1.	H T O	Th H T O	Th H T O	Th H T O

a
```
  H | T | O
    | 2 | 2
  × | 4 | 0
    | 0 | 0  ←
+ 8 | 8 | 0
  8 | 8 | 0
```

b
```
Th| H | T | O
  |   | 5 | 7
× |   | 8 | 0
```

c
```
Th| H | T | O
  |   | 6 | 3
× |   | 7 | 0
```

d
```
Th| H | T | O
  |   | 8 | 4
× |   | 6 | 0
```

2.

```
    3 0
  × 4 0
```

```
    7 0
  × 6 0
```

```
  5 8 0
  × 3 0
```

```
  4,0 0 6
  ×    5 0
```

Line up the digits. Then find the products.

	a	*b*	*c*

3. 430 × 70 = _____   2,470 × 90 = _____   3,000 × 80 = _____

```
  430
× 70
```

Multiplication of Three-digit Numbers

To multiply by three-digit numbers, multiply by the ones first.
Then multiply by the tens and hundreds. Then add these
three partial products.

Find: 342 × 103

Multiply by 3 ones. Regroup.	Write a zero place holder. Multiply by 0 tens.	Write two zero place holders. Multiply by 1 hundred.	Add the partial products.

Th	H	T	O
	1		
3	4	2
×	1	0	3
1,	0	2	6

Th	H	T	O
	3	4	2
×	1	0	3
1,	0	2	6
0	0	0	0

TTh	Th	H	T	O
		3	4	2
×		1	0	3
	1,	0	2	6
	0	0	0	0
3	4,	2	0	0

TTh	Th	H	T	O
		3	4	2
×		1	0	3
	1,	0	2	6
	0	0	0	0
+3	4,	2	0	0
3	5,	2	2	6

Multiply.

	a	b	c	d
1.	361 ×313 1,083 3,610 +108,300 112,993	358 ×637	507 ×383	870 ×647
2.	950 ×603	621 ×583	932 ×785	400 ×803

Line up the digits. Then find the products.

	a	b	c
3.	783 × 342 = _____	850 × 330 = _____	742 × 582 = _____

783
×342

Estimation of Products

To estimate products, round each **factor**.
Then multiply the rounded factors.

Estimate: 72 × 35

> Round each factor to the greatest place value.
> Multiply.
>
> $$\begin{array}{r} 7\,2 \rightarrow \quad 7\,0 \\ \times\,3\,5 \rightarrow \times\quad 4\,0 \\ \hline 2,8\,0\,0 \end{array}$$

Estimate: 369 × 21

> Round each factor to the greatest place value.
> Multiply.
>
> $$\begin{array}{r} 3\,6\,9 \rightarrow \quad 4\,0\,0 \\ \times\quad 2\,1 \rightarrow \times\quad 2\,0 \\ \hline 8,0\,0\,0 \end{array}$$

Estimate the products.

	a	b	c	d

1.
$$\begin{array}{r} 3\,1 \rightarrow \quad 3\,0 \\ \times\,4\,6 \rightarrow \times\,5\,0 \\ \hline 1,5\,0\,0 \end{array}$$
$$\begin{array}{r} 2\,2 \rightarrow \\ \times\,5\,3 \rightarrow \\ \hline \end{array}$$
$$\begin{array}{r} 7\,4 \rightarrow \\ \times\,5\,5 \rightarrow \\ \hline \end{array}$$
$$\begin{array}{r} 8\,6 \rightarrow \\ \times\,9\,1 \rightarrow \\ \hline \end{array}$$

2.
$$\begin{array}{r} 6\,5 \rightarrow \\ \times\,2\,1 \rightarrow \\ \hline \end{array}$$
$$\begin{array}{r} 4\,7 \rightarrow \\ \times\,3\,2 \rightarrow \\ \hline \end{array}$$
$$\begin{array}{r} 3\,9 \rightarrow \\ \times\,6\,3 \rightarrow \\ \hline \end{array}$$
$$\begin{array}{r} 5\,9 \rightarrow \\ \times\,7\,7 \rightarrow \\ \hline \end{array}$$

3.
$$\begin{array}{r} 2\,7\,6 \rightarrow \\ \times\quad 4\,5 \rightarrow \\ \hline \end{array}$$
$$\begin{array}{r} 6\,7\,1 \rightarrow \\ \times\quad 9\,3 \rightarrow \\ \hline \end{array}$$
$$\begin{array}{r} 2\,5\,3 \rightarrow \\ \times\quad 8\,5 \rightarrow \\ \hline \end{array}$$
$$\begin{array}{r} 7\,1\,2 \rightarrow \\ \times\quad 9\,7 \rightarrow \\ \hline \end{array}$$

Line up the digits. Then estimate the products.

	a	b	c

4. 67 × 23 _____   94 × 52 _____   749 × 28 _____

$$\begin{array}{r} 6\,7 \rightarrow \quad 7\,0 \\ \times\,2\,3 \rightarrow \times\,2\,0 \\ \hline \end{array}$$

One-digit and Two-digit Divisors with Remainders

To divide by a one-digit divisor, first choose a **trial quotient.** Then multiply and subtract. Remember, if your trial quotient is too large or too small, try another number.

To divide by a two-digit divisor, first choose a trial quotient. Multiply and subtract. Then write the remainder in the quotient.

Find: 739 ÷ 22

Divide.	Multiply and subtract.	Multiply and subtract.	Check:

H | T | O
 $22\overline{)7\,3\,9}$
 	
 $7 < 22$
 	
 22 does not go into 7.
	H | T | O
	    3
	 $22\overline{)7\,3\,9}$
	 $-6\,6\downarrow$
	    7 | 9
	
	 $2\overline{)7}$ is about 3.
	 So, $22\overline{)73}$ is about 3.
		H | T | O
		    3\,3 R13
		 $22\overline{)7\,3\,9}$
		 $-6\,6$
		   7 | 9
		 $-6\,6$
		   1 | 3
		
		 $2\overline{)7}$ is about 3.
		 So, $22\overline{)79}$ is about 3.
			33
			 ×22
			 726
			 + 13
			 739

Divide.

       a   *b*   *c*   *d*

1.   3 4 R1
   $2\overline{)6\,9}$ $6\overline{)5\,6\,8}$ $3\overline{)2\,8\,9}$ $5\overline{)2\,7\,4}$
   $-6\downarrow$
    0 9
   $-\,8$
     1

2.
  $27\overline{)4,5\,2\,1}$ $84\overline{)5,9\,3\,4}$ $41\overline{)5,2\,1\,9}$ $62\overline{)8,6\,9\,4}$

Set up the problems. Then find the quotients.

                a   *b*   *c*

3. 461 ÷ 3 = _____   784 ÷ 5 = _____   32,692 ÷ 12 = _____

   $3\overline{)461}$

Dividing by Multiples of 10

To divide by multiples of ten, choose a trial quotient.
Then multiply and subtract.

Find: 570 ÷ 40

Divide.	Multiply and subtract.	Multiply and subtract.	Check:

Divide.

```
        H | T | O
40)5 | 7 | 0
```

5 < 40

40 does not
go into 5.

Multiply and subtract.

```
        H | T | O
            1
40)5 | 7 | 0
   -4 | 0 ↓
     1 | 7 | 0
```

Think: 4)5 is about 1.
So, 40)57 is about 1.
Put the 1 above the 7.

Multiply and subtract.

```
        H | T | O
            1 | 4  R10
40)5 | 7 | 0
   -4 | 0
     1 | 7 | 0
   -1 | 6 | 0
         1 | 0
```

Think: 4)17 is about 4.
So, 40)170 is about 4.

Check:

```
    14
  ×40
  560
 + 10
  570
```

Divide.

	a	b	c	d

1.

```
        1  1  R 39
  40)4 7 9
    -4 0 ↓
       7 9
      -4 0
       3 9
```

b 80)4 3 0

c 20)3 6 8

d 10)4 9 7

2.

a 50)6,3 6 0

b 20)3,8 5 6

c 40)5,9 0 0

d 80)7,8 5 0

Set up the problems. Then find the quotients.

a
3. 3,875 ÷ 70 = _____

70)3,875

b
5,183 ÷ 20 = _____

19

Trial Quotient: Too Large or Too Small

When you divide, you may have to try several quotients.
Use rounding to choose a trial quotient. Then multiply and subtract.
If it is too large or too small, try again.

Find: 672 ÷ 24

Use rounding to choose a trial quotient.	Multiply and subtract.	Try a smaller number. Multiply and subtract.	Finish the problem.
$24\overline{)6\ 7\ 2}$	$\dfrac{3}{24\overline{)6\ 7\ 2}}$ $-7\ 2$	$\dfrac{2}{24\overline{)6\ 7\ 2}}$ $-4\ 8$ $\ \ 1\ 9$	$\dfrac{2\ 8}{24\overline{)6\ 7\ 2}}$ $-4\ 8\ \downarrow$ $\ \ 1\ 9\ 2$ $-1\ 9\ 2$ $\ \ 0$
Think: 24 rounds to 20. $\dfrac{3}{2\overline{)6}}$ So, $24\overline{)67}$ is about 3.	Since 72 > 67, 3 is too large.	Since 19 < 24, 2 is correct.	

Find: 675 ÷ 15

$15\overline{)6\ 7\ 5}$	$\dfrac{3}{15\overline{)6\ 7\ 5}}$ $-4\ 5$ $\ \ 2\ 2$	$\dfrac{4}{15\overline{)6\ 7\ 5}}$ $-6\ 0$ $\ \ \ \ 7$	$\dfrac{4\ 5}{15\overline{)6\ 7\ 5}}$ $-6\ 0\ \downarrow$ $\ \ \ \ 7\ 5$ $-7\ 5$ $\ \ \ \ \ 0$
Think: 15 rounds to 20. $\dfrac{3}{2\overline{)6}}$ So, $15\overline{)67}$ is about 3.	Since 22 > 15, 3 is too small.	Since 7 < 15, 4 is correct.	

Write _too large, too small,_ or _correct_ for each trial quotient.
Then write the correct trial quotient.

	a			*b*	
1. $\dfrac{2}{25\overline{)4\ 7\ 5}}$	_too large_ _____ _____ 1		$\dfrac{3}{15\overline{)6\ 8\ 2}}$	_____ _____	
2. $\dfrac{4}{61\overline{)2,4\ 1\ 9}}$	_____ _____		$\dfrac{3}{42\overline{)1,2\ 5\ 3}}$	_____ _____	
3. $\dfrac{8}{54\overline{)4\ 1,2\ 4\ 9}}$	_____ _____		$\dfrac{3}{27\overline{)6\ 5,4\ 8\ 7}}$	_____ _____	

Zeros in Quotients

When you cannot divide, write a zero in the quotient as a place holder.

Find: 2,430 ÷ 4

Divide.	Multiply and subtract.	Multiply and subtract.	Multiply and subtract.

Divide.

```
   Th | H | T | O
   4)2,| 4 | 3 | 0

   2 < 4

   4 does not
   go into 2.
```

Multiply and subtract.

```
       | 6 |   |
   Th | H | T | O
   4)2,| 4 | 3 | 0
    − 2| 4 |   |
       | 0 | 3 |

        6
      4)24
```

Multiply and subtract.

```
       | 6 | 0 |      ← Write a zero
   Th | H | T | O        in the quotient
   4)2,| 4 | 3 | 0       as a place
    − 2| 4 |   |          holder.
       | 0 | 3 |
    −  |   | 0 |
       |   | 3 | 0

        0
      4)3
```

Multiply and subtract.

```
       | 6 | 0 | 7  R 2
   Th | H | T | O
   4)2,| 4 | 3 | 0
    − 2| 4 |   |
       | 0 | 3 |
    −  |   | 0 |
       |   | 3 | 0
    −  |   | 2 | 8
       |   |   | 2
```

Divide.

	a	b	c	d

1.
```
     3 0 4
   2)6 0 8
   −6
    0 0
   −  0
      0 8
   −  8
      0
```
b. 4)4 2 8

c. 9)1,8 4 5

d. 7)1,4 6 3

2.   81)4 1,0 6 7   97)5 8,3 9 4   89)1 8,5 1 2

Estimation of Quotients

To estimate quotients, round the numbers to use basic division facts.

Estimate: $243 \div 5$

Round the dividend until you can use a basic fact. Divide.

$5\overline{)243}$ $\qquad$ $243 \div 5$

Think: $25 \div 5 = 5$ $\qquad\downarrow\qquad\downarrow$

$\qquad\qquad\qquad 250 \div 5 = 50$

Estimate: $424 \div 61$

Round the dividend and the divisor until you can use a basic fact. Divide.

$61\overline{)424}$ $\qquad$ $424 \div 61$

Think: $42 \div 6 = 7$ $\qquad\downarrow\qquad\downarrow$

$\qquad\qquad\qquad 420 \div 60 = 7$

Round the dividends to estimate the quotients.

	a	b	c

1. $3\overline{)1\ 2\ 1} \rightarrow 3\overset{4\ 0}{\overline{)1\ 2\ 0}}$ $\qquad$ $4\overline{)2\ 8\ 4} \rightarrow$ $\qquad$ $8\overline{)7\ 1\ 2} \rightarrow$

2. $8\overline{)5,\ 7\ 4\ 7} \rightarrow$ $\qquad$ $7\overline{)2,3\ 1\ 2} \rightarrow$ $\qquad$ $5\overline{)2,9\ 3\ 4} \rightarrow$

Round the dividends and the divisors to estimate the quotients.

	a	b	c

3. $23\overline{)7\ 8\ 3} \rightarrow$ $\qquad$ $35\overline{)8\ 0\ 5} \rightarrow$ $\qquad$ $29\overline{)5\ 9\ 7} \rightarrow$

4. $42\overline{)8\ 0\ 7} \rightarrow$ $\qquad$ $53\overline{)7\ 5\ 4} \rightarrow$ $\qquad$ $84\overline{)6\ 4\ 4} \rightarrow$

Problem-Solving Method: Choose an Operation

Pythons are the longest snakes in the world. The largest python was found in Indonesia in 1912. It was 396 inches long. Since there are 12 inches in 1 foot, how many feet long was the python?

Understand the problem.

- **What do you want to know?**
  the length of the python in feet

- **What information is given?**
  It was 396 inches long.
  There are 12 inches in 1 foot.

Plan how to solve it.

- **What method can you use?**
  You can choose the operation needed to solve it.

Unequal groups	Equal groups
Add to combine unequal groups.	**Multiply** to combine equal groups.
Subtract to separate into unequal groups.	**Divide** to separate into equal groups.

Solve it.

- **How can you use this method to solve the problem?**
  Since you need to separate the total 396 inches into equal groups of 12 inches, you should divide to find *how many equal groups*.

$$
\begin{array}{r}
33 \\
12\overline{)396} \\
-36\downarrow \\
\hline
36 \\
-36 \\
\hline
0
\end{array}
$$

- **What is the answer?**
  The python was 33 feet long.

Look back and check your answer.

- **Is your answer reasonable?**
  You can check division with multiplication.

$$
\begin{array}{r}
33 \\
\times\ 12 \\
\hline
396
\end{array}
$$

The product matches the dividend.

The answer is reasonable.

**Choose an operation to solve each problem.
Then solve the problem.**

1. North Dakota covers 70,704 square miles. South Dakota covers 77,121 square miles. How much land do the Dakotas cover in all?

Operation _____

Answer _____

2. In 1967, 61,946 people attended the first Super Bowl. In 1968, 75,546 people attended. How many more people went to the second Super Bowl than the first?

Operation _____

Answer _____

3. It is 385 miles between San Francisco and Los Angeles. Driving at 55 miles per hour, how long will the trip take?

Operation _____

Answer _____

4. Charles worked 40 hours this week and made $520. How much did he earn each hour?

Operation _____

Answer _____

5. The average alligator is 180 inches long. How many feet long is an average alligator? (1 foot = 12 inches)

Operation _____

Answer _____

UNIT 1 Review

Write the place name for the 7 in each number.

         a   *b*

1. 67,302,284 _____   528,972,343 _____

Write each number using digits. Insert commas where needed.

2. one million, fifty thousand, forty-five _____

3. two million, seven thousand, six _____

Compare. Write <, >, or =.

        a   *b*   *c*

4. 590 _____ 462   57,098 _____ 650,245   1,202,865 _____ 36,248,762

Write in order from least to greatest.

5. 702   722   720   _____

6. 6,789   9,789   9,786   _____

Add or subtract.

	a	*b*	*c*
7.	$\begin{array}{r} 5\ 4\ 2 \\ +\ \ \ 2\ 1 \\ \hline \end{array}$	$\begin{array}{r} 9\ 3\ 4 \\ -5\ 4\ 7 \\ \hline \end{array}$	$\begin{array}{r} 9\ 9,2\ 4\ 7 \\ -7\ 5,4\ 2\ 1 \\ \hline \end{array}$
8.	$\begin{array}{r} 5\ 8\ 9,3\ 2\ 1 \\ -2\ 5\ 7,4\ 3\ 2 \\ \hline \end{array}$	$\begin{array}{r} 8\ 9,4\ 9\ 2 \\ 5\ 4,9\ 8\ 2 \\ +4\ 2,5\ 6\ 8 \\ \hline \end{array}$	$\begin{array}{r} 5\ 3\ 4,9\ 7\ 5 \\ -2\ 3\ 8,5\ 7\ 3 \\ \hline \end{array}$

Estimate the sums or differences.

	a	*b*	*c*
9.	$\begin{array}{r} 5\ 4 \longrightarrow \\ +5\ 6\ 2 \longrightarrow \\ \hline \end{array}$	$\begin{array}{r} 4\ 5\ 3 \longrightarrow \\ -2\ 9\ 8 \longrightarrow \\ \hline \end{array}$	$\begin{array}{r} 7\ 6\ 4 \longrightarrow \\ +2\ 3\ 4 \longrightarrow \\ \hline \end{array}$
10.	$\begin{array}{r} 3\ 2,3\ 4\ 2 \longrightarrow \\ +7\ 6,9\ 6\ 4 \longrightarrow \\ \hline \end{array}$	$\begin{array}{r} 7\ 2,4\ 3\ 2 \longrightarrow \\ -4\ 5,8\ 6\ 4 \longrightarrow \\ \hline \end{array}$	$\begin{array}{r} 1,1\ 5\ 5 \longrightarrow \\ +2\ 5,6\ 7\ 7 \longrightarrow \\ \hline \end{array}$

UNIT 1 Review

Multiply.

	a	b	c	d
11.	46 × 3	47 × 4	344 × 6	89 ×56
12.	468 × 25	637 × 75	8,544 × 34	34,864 × 50
13.	53,056 × 35	506 ×763	553 ×602	900 ×500

Divide.

	a	b	c	d
14.	8)675	4)890	6)7,653	5)67,045
15.	34)758	60)573	26)5,700	70)8,402
16.	34)86,465	83)64,908	80)56,396	51)76,998

Estimate the products or quotients.

	a	b	c
17.	57 → ×79 →	8)435 →	76 → ×21 →
18.	7)5,632 →	683 → × 49 →	81)315 →

26

UNIT 1 Review

Guess and check to solve each problem.

19. Shawn and Andy made 86 cupcakes in all. Shawn made 10 more than Andy. How many cupcakes did they each make?

Answer _____

20. Gail has eight United States coins. Their total value is 93 cents. What coins does she have?

Answer _____

Choose an operation to solve each problem. Then solve the problem.

21. John has 123 more baseball cards than Mark. Mark has 679 cards. How many baseball cards does John have?

Operation _____

Answer _____

22. The *Daily News* packs 458 bundles of newspapers every day. Each bundle has 250 papers. How many papers does the *Daily News* pack each day?

Operation _____

Answer _____

23. There were 1,291 cars in the parking lot this morning. By 5:00 P.M., 138 cars had left. How many cars were still in the parking lot?

Operation _____

Answer _____

Meaning of Fractions

A **fraction** names part of a whole. This circle has 4 equal parts. Each part is $\frac{1}{4}$ of the circle.

Three of the equal parts are shaded yellow.

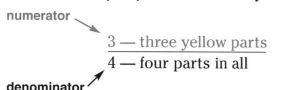

numerator

3 — three yellow parts
4 — four parts in all

denominator

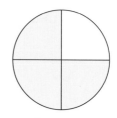

We read $\frac{3}{4}$ as **three-fourths**.

A fraction also names parts of a group. Two of the five cookies are chocolate chip.

2 — two chocolate chip cookies
5 — five cookies in all

Two-fifths are chocolate chip.

Write the fraction and the word name for the part that is shaded.

a	b	c

1.

$\frac{2}{3}$ or _two-thirds_   _____ or _____   _____ or _____

2.

_____ or _____   _____ or _____   _____ or _____

Write the fraction for the word name.

           a   b   c

3. three-eighths $\frac{3}{8}$ one-fourth _____   four-fifths _____

Write the word name for the fraction.

           a   b   c

4. $\frac{5}{6}$ _five-sixths_ $\frac{2}{7}$ _____ $\frac{7}{8}$ _____

Improper Fractions and Mixed Numbers

An **improper** fraction is a fraction with a numerator that is greater than or equal to the denominator.

$\frac{6}{6}$, $\frac{12}{3}$, and $\frac{8}{5}$ are improper fractions.

An improper fraction can be written as a whole or mixed number.

A **mixed number** is a whole number and a fraction.

$1\frac{3}{4}$ is a mixed number.

A mixed number can be written as an improper fraction.

Write $\frac{6}{6}$ and $\frac{12}{3}$ as whole numbers.

Write $\frac{8}{5}$ as a mixed number.

Write $1\frac{3}{4}$ as an improper fraction.

Divide the numerator by the denominator.

$$6\overline{)6}^{\;1} \qquad \frac{6}{6} = 1$$

$$3\overline{)12}^{\;4} \qquad \frac{12}{3} = 4$$

Divide the numerator by the denominator. Write the remainder as a fraction by writing the remainder over the divisor.

$$5\overline{)8}^{\;1\frac{3}{5}}$$
$$\underline{-5}$$
$$3$$

$$\frac{8}{5} = 1\frac{3}{5}$$

Multiply the whole number by the denominator. Add this product to the numerator. Then write the sum over the denominator.

$$1\frac{3}{4} = \frac{1 \times 4 + 3}{4} = \frac{4 + 3}{4} = \frac{7}{4}$$

$$1\frac{3}{4} = \frac{7}{4}$$

Write as a whole number.

	a	b	c	d
1.	$\frac{16}{4} = \underline{\quad 4 \quad}$	$\frac{15}{5} = \underline{\qquad}$	$\frac{28}{4} = \underline{\qquad}$	$\frac{48}{6} = \underline{\qquad}$

Write as a mixed number.

	a	b	c	d
2.	$\frac{15}{4} = \underline{\quad 3\frac{3}{4} \quad}$	$\frac{21}{5} = \underline{\qquad}$	$\frac{23}{6} = \underline{\qquad}$	$\frac{7}{2} = \underline{\qquad}$

Write as an improper fraction.

	a	b	c	d
3.	$2\frac{7}{10} = \underline{\quad \frac{27}{10} \quad}$	$8\frac{1}{3} = \underline{\qquad}$	$5\frac{1}{6} = \underline{\qquad}$	$3\frac{2}{5} = \underline{\qquad}$

Equivalent Fractions

To add or subtract fractions, you might need to use **equivalent fractions**, or fractions that have the same value.

To change a fraction to an equivalent fraction in **higher terms**, multiply the numerator and the denominator by the same number.

Rewrite $\frac{3}{4}$ with 8 as the denominator.

Compare the denominators.	Multiply both the numerator and the denominator by 2.
$\frac{3}{4} = \frac{}{8}$ Think: $4 \times 2 = 8$	$\frac{3}{4} = \frac{3 \times 2}{4 \times 2} = \frac{6}{8}$

You can also use the **lowest common denominator (LCD)** to write equivalent fractions.

Use the LCD to write equivalent fractions for $\frac{1}{2}$ and $\frac{2}{5}$.

List several multiples for each denominator.	Find the LCD. It is the smallest number that appears on both lists.	Write equivalent fractions.
Multiples of 2: 2 4 6 8 10 12 Multiples of 5: 5 10 15 20 25	The LCD of $\frac{1}{2}$ and $\frac{2}{5}$ is 10.	$\frac{1}{2} = \frac{1 \times 5}{2 \times 5} = \frac{5}{10}$ $\frac{2}{5} = \frac{2 \times 2}{5 \times 2} = \frac{4}{10}$

Rewrite each fraction as an equivalent fraction in higher terms.

	a	b	c	d
1.	$\frac{5}{8} = \frac{5 \times 2}{8 \times 2} = \frac{10}{16}$	$\frac{3}{4} = \frac{}{16}$	$\frac{2}{3} = \frac{}{12}$	$\frac{2}{5} = \frac{}{10}$
2.	$\frac{3}{5} = \frac{}{25}$	$\frac{2}{5} = \frac{}{15}$	$\frac{5}{6} = \frac{}{24}$	$\frac{7}{8} = \frac{}{16}$

Use the LCD to write equivalent fractions.

	a	b	c	d
3.	$\frac{1}{3} = \frac{1 \times 2}{3 \times 2} = \frac{2}{6}$ $\frac{1}{2} = \frac{1 \times 3}{2 \times 3} = \frac{3}{6}$	$\frac{1}{2} =$ $\frac{3}{5} =$	$\frac{7}{10} =$ $\frac{3}{4} =$	$\frac{2}{3} =$ $\frac{5}{7} =$

Simplifying Fractions

When you find the answer to a problem with fractions, you might need to change the fraction to an equivalent fraction in simplest terms. To **simplify** a fraction, divide both the numerator and the denominator by the same greatest number possible.

Simplify: $\frac{8}{14}$

Consider the numerator and denominator.

$\frac{8}{14} =$

Think: 14 can be divided by 7 but 8 cannot.
8 can be divided by 4 but 14 cannot.
Both 14 and 8 can be divided by 2.

Divide the numerator and the denominator by 2.

$\frac{8}{14} = \frac{8 \div 2}{14 \div 2} = \frac{4}{7}$

A fraction is in simplest terms when 1 is the only number that divides both the numerator and the denominator evenly.

The fraction $\frac{4}{7}$ is in simplest terms.

Simplify.

	a	b	c	d
1.	$\frac{9}{21} = \frac{9 \div 3}{21 \div 3} = \frac{3}{7}$	$\frac{2}{10} =$	$\frac{4}{12} =$	$\frac{12}{18} =$
2.	$\frac{4}{6} =$	$\frac{2}{8} =$	$\frac{8}{20} =$	$\frac{10}{12} =$
3.	$\frac{45}{45} =$	$\frac{9}{15} =$	$\frac{2}{12} =$	$\frac{6}{14} =$
4.	$\frac{9}{12} =$	$\frac{3}{9} =$	$\frac{10}{20} =$	$\frac{6}{8} =$
5.	$\frac{9}{21} =$	$\frac{2}{20} =$	$\frac{4}{36} =$	$\frac{12}{24} =$

Addition and Subtraction of Fractions with Like Denominators

To add or subtract fractions with like denominators, add or subtract the numerators. Use the same denominator. Simplify the answer.

Remember,

- to simplify an improper fraction, write it as a whole number or a mixed number.

- to simplify a proper fraction, write it in simplest terms.

Find: $\frac{9}{10} + \frac{8}{10}$

Add the numerators.	Use the same denominator.
$\frac{9}{10}$	$\frac{9}{10}$
$+\frac{8}{10}$	$+\frac{8}{10}$
$\overline{17}$	$\frac{17}{10} = 1\frac{7}{10}$
	Simplify the answer.

Find: $\frac{11}{12} - \frac{7}{12}$

Subtract the numerators.	Use the same denominator.
$\frac{11}{12}$	$\frac{11}{12}$
$-\frac{7}{12}$	$-\frac{7}{12}$
$\overline{4}$	$\frac{4}{12} = \frac{1}{3}$
	Simplify the answer.

Add. Simplify.

	a	b	c	d	e
1.	$\frac{3}{8}$ $+\frac{1}{8}$ $\frac{4}{8} = \frac{1}{2}$	$\frac{3}{10}$ $+\frac{1}{10}$	$\frac{2}{6}$ $+\frac{1}{6}$	$\frac{5}{16}$ $+\frac{1}{16}$	$\frac{7}{16}$ $+\frac{3}{16}$
2.	$\frac{5}{6}$ $+\frac{2}{6}$	$\frac{7}{8}$ $+\frac{5}{8}$	$\frac{8}{10}$ $+\frac{5}{10}$	$\frac{4}{5}$ $+\frac{3}{5}$	$\frac{11}{12}$ $+\frac{6}{12}$

Subtract. Simplify.

	a	b	c	d	e
3.	$\frac{5}{8}$ $-\frac{3}{8}$ $\frac{2}{8} = \frac{1}{4}$	$\frac{7}{10}$ $-\frac{3}{10}$	$\frac{7}{12}$ $-\frac{5}{12}$	$\frac{5}{8}$ $-\frac{1}{8}$	$\frac{15}{16}$ $-\frac{3}{16}$

Addition of Fractions with Different Denominators

To add fractions with different denominators, first rewrite the fractions as equivalent fractions with like denominators. Then add the numerators and simplify the answer.

Find: $\frac{1}{6} + \frac{1}{3}$

Write equivalent fractions with like denominators.

$$\frac{1}{6} = \frac{1}{6}$$
$$+\frac{1}{3} = \frac{2}{6}$$

Remember,

$$\frac{1}{3} = \frac{1 \times 2}{3 \times 2} = \frac{2}{6}$$

Add the numerators. Use the same denominator.

$$\frac{1}{6} = \frac{1}{6}$$
$$+\frac{1}{3} = \frac{2}{6}$$
$$\frac{3}{6} = \frac{1}{2} \quad \text{Simplify the answer.}$$

Add. Simplify.

	a	b	c	d
1.	$\frac{1}{5} = \frac{2}{10}$ $\quad +\frac{1}{10} = \frac{1}{10}$ $\quad \frac{3}{10}$	$\frac{1}{4}$ $\quad +\frac{1}{2}$	$\frac{1}{2}$ $\quad +\frac{3}{8}$	$\frac{3}{4}$ $\quad +\frac{1}{8}$
2.	$\frac{3}{4}$ $\quad +\frac{1}{12}$	$\frac{1}{2}$ $\quad +\frac{1}{6}$	$\frac{1}{10}$ $\quad +\frac{1}{2}$	$\frac{5}{12}$ $\quad +\frac{1}{4}$
3.	$\frac{1}{2}$ $\quad +\frac{3}{10}$	$\frac{5}{16}$ $\quad +\frac{1}{4}$	$\frac{1}{2}$ $\quad +\frac{5}{12}$	$\frac{4}{9}$ $\quad +\frac{1}{3}$

Set up the problems. Then find the sums. Simplify.

a	b	c

4. $\frac{1}{3} + \frac{2}{9} =$ _____

$\frac{1}{3}$
$+\frac{2}{9}$

$\frac{2}{8} + \frac{1}{24} =$ _____

$\frac{3}{6} + \frac{2}{18} =$ _____

Addition of Fractions Using the Least Common Denominator

Find: $\frac{1}{2} + \frac{3}{5}$

Write equivalent fractions with like denominators. Use the LCD.

$$\frac{1}{2} = \frac{1 \times 5}{2 \times 5} = \frac{5}{10}$$
$$+\frac{3}{5} = \frac{3 \times 2}{5 \times 2} = \frac{6}{10}$$

Add the numerators. Use the same denominator.

$$\frac{1}{2} = \frac{5}{10}$$
$$+\frac{3}{5} = \frac{6}{10}$$
$$\frac{11}{10} = 1\frac{1}{10} \quad \text{Simplify the answer.}$$

Add. Simplify.

	a	b	c	d
1.	$\frac{1}{2} = \frac{3}{6}$	$\frac{3}{7}$	$\frac{2}{3}$	$\frac{2}{5}$
	$+\frac{2}{3} = \frac{4}{6}$	$+\frac{1}{2}$	$+\frac{3}{4}$	$+\frac{7}{9}$
	$\frac{7}{6} = 1\frac{1}{6}$			

	a	b	c	d
2.	$\frac{2}{3}$	$\frac{3}{8}$	$\frac{4}{5}$	$\frac{2}{7}$
	$+\frac{7}{8}$	$+\frac{5}{6}$	$+\frac{2}{3}$	$+\frac{2}{3}$

	a	b	c	d
3.	$\frac{5}{6}$	$\frac{1}{3}$	$\frac{5}{6}$	$\frac{1}{2}$
	$+\frac{3}{4}$	$+\frac{3}{10}$	$+\frac{3}{5}$	$+\frac{5}{9}$

Set up the problems. Then find the sums. Simplify.

a	b	c
4. $\frac{3}{7} + \frac{1}{4} =$ _____	$\frac{4}{5} + \frac{7}{11} =$ _____	$\frac{1}{7} + \frac{2}{8} =$ _____

$\frac{3}{7}$
$+\frac{1}{4}$

Problem-Solving Method: Make a Graph

Coach Esteves took a survey to choose the team's mascot. Of the 24 players, $\frac{1}{3}$ chose Bulldogs, $\frac{1}{2}$ chose Bears, and $\frac{1}{6}$ chose Lions. How can he present the results of the survey to the team?

Understand the problem.

- **What do you want to know?**
  how to present the results of the survey

- **What information is given?**
  24 people voted: $\frac{1}{3}$ for Bulldogs, $\frac{1}{2}$ for Bears, and $\frac{1}{6}$ for Lions.

Plan how to solve it.

- **What method can you use?**
  You can make a circle graph to show the data as parts of a whole.

Solve it.

- **How can you use this method to solve the problem?**
  Use a circle divided into 24 equal parts to represent the whole team. Then shade and label the number of votes for each mascot. (Remember, to find $\frac{1}{2}$ of 8, divide 8 by 2. $\frac{1}{2}$ of $8 = 8 \div 2 = 4$)

TEAM MASCOT VOTE

Mascot	Fraction of All the Votes	Number of Votes
Bulldogs	$\frac{1}{3}$ of 24 =	8
Bears	$\frac{1}{2}$ of 24 =	12
Lions	$\frac{1}{6}$ of 24 =	4

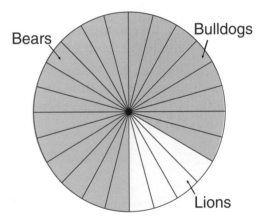

- **What is the answer?**
  The results of the survey can be presented in a circle graph.

Look back and check your answer.

- **Is your answer reasonable?**
  The whole circle represents the whole survey—24 votes.
  The sum of the number of votes in each section should be 24.

  8 + 12 + 4 = 24

  The answer is reasonable.

Make a graph to solve each problem.

1. Jamal has 28 CDs in his collection. $\frac{1}{4}$ of the CDs are Rock, $\frac{1}{2}$ are R&B, and $\frac{1}{4}$ are Jazz. Make a circle graph to show Jamal's CD collection.

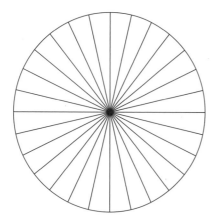

2. Twelve students voted for their favorite ice cream. Vanilla got $\frac{1}{6}$ of the votes, chocolate got $\frac{2}{3}$, and strawberry got $\frac{1}{6}$. Make a circle graph to show how many students voted for each flavor.

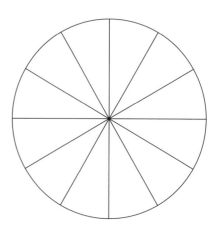

3. Laura worked 8 hours today. She spent $\frac{1}{2}$ the time in meetings, $\frac{1}{8}$ on the phone, and the rest of the time on the computer. Make a circle graph to show how Laura spent her work day.

4. In the United States, $\frac{7}{10}$ of the population has brown hair, $\frac{3}{20}$ has blonde hair, $\frac{1}{10}$ has black hair, and $\frac{1}{20}$ are redheads. Make a circle graph to show the hair color of an average group of 20 people in the United States.

Adding Mixed Numbers, Whole Numbers, and Fractions

To add mixed numbers, whole numbers, and fractions, first check for unlike denominators. Write mixed numbers and fractions as equivalent fractions with like denominators. Add the fractions. Then add the whole numbers and simplify.

Find: $2\frac{7}{12} + \frac{1}{4}$

Write the fractions with like denominators.	Add the fractions.	Add the whole numbers.	Simplify.
$2\frac{7}{12} = 2\frac{7}{12}$ $+ \ \ \frac{1}{4} = \ \ \frac{3}{12}$	$2\frac{7}{12} = 2\frac{7}{12}$ $+ \ \ \frac{1}{4} = \ \ \frac{3}{12}$ $\overline{\qquad \frac{10}{12}}$	$2\frac{7}{12} = 2\frac{7}{12}$ $+ \ \ \frac{1}{4} = \ \ \frac{3}{12}$ $\overline{\quad 2\frac{10}{12}}$	$2\frac{10}{12} = 2\frac{5}{6}$

Remember, $\frac{1}{4} = \frac{3}{12}$.
They are equivalent fractions.

Add. Simplify.

	a	b	c	d
1.	$4\frac{1}{2} = 4\frac{2}{4}$ $+ \ \ \frac{1}{4} = \ \ \frac{1}{4}$ $\overline{\quad 4\frac{3}{4}}$	$\frac{1}{2}$ $+ \ 8\frac{1}{8}$	$6\frac{1}{4}$ $+ \ \ \ \frac{1}{8}$	$\frac{1}{2}$ $+ \ 9\frac{3}{8}$
2.	$1\,2\frac{1}{3}$ $+ \ \ 9\frac{1}{6}$	$8\frac{1}{2}$ $+ \ 9\frac{1}{10}$	$1\,2\frac{1}{5}$ $+ \ \ 7\frac{1}{10}$	$6\frac{1}{3}$ $+ \ 8\frac{1}{9}$
3.	$\frac{1}{3}$ $+ \ 2\frac{1}{4}$	$3\frac{1}{4}$ $+ \ \ \frac{2}{3}$	$7\frac{1}{2}$ $+ \ \ \frac{1}{3}$	$\frac{3}{8}$ $+ \ 1\frac{1}{7}$
4.	$5\frac{1}{8}$ $+ \ 6\frac{1}{6}$	$8\frac{1}{4}$ $+ \ 9\frac{1}{3}$	$4\frac{2}{5}$ $+ \ 7\frac{1}{2}$	$7\frac{1}{2}$ $+ \ 8\frac{3}{10}$

Adding Mixed Numbers with Large Sums

When adding mixed numbers, whole numbers, and fractions, your sum might contain an improper fraction. To regroup a sum that contains an improper fraction, first write the improper fraction as a mixed number. Then add and simplify.

Find: $5\frac{1}{3} + \frac{5}{7}$

Write the fractions with like denominators. Add.

$$5\frac{1}{3} = 5\frac{7}{21}$$
$$+ \ \frac{5}{7} = \ \frac{15}{21}$$
$$\overline{\qquad\quad 5\frac{22}{21}}$$

The sum $5\frac{22}{21}$ contains an improper fraction. To regroup, write the improper fraction as a mixed number.

$$\frac{22}{21} = 1\frac{1}{21}$$

Then add.

$$5\frac{22}{21} = 5 + 1\frac{1}{21} = 6\frac{1}{21}$$

Add. Simplify.

	a	b	c	d
1.	$4\frac{1}{2} = 4\frac{3}{6}$ $+ \ \frac{5}{6} = \frac{5}{6}$ $\overline{\quad 4\frac{8}{6} = 5\frac{1}{3}}$	$9\frac{2}{5}$ $+ \ \frac{5}{6}$	$3\frac{2}{3}$ $+ \ \frac{8}{9}$	$\frac{3}{7}$ $+ 6\frac{7}{8}$
2.	$2\frac{3}{4}$ $+ 7\frac{5}{6}$	$9\frac{1}{3}$ $+ 4\frac{7}{9}$	$10\frac{5}{7}$ $+ 7\frac{9}{11}$	$1\frac{1}{2}$ $+ 9\frac{11}{12}$
3.	$9\frac{2}{3}$ $+ \ \frac{3}{4}$	$7\frac{3}{9}$ $+ \ \frac{1}{2}$	$10\frac{9}{10}$ $+ \ \frac{2}{5}$	$8\frac{1}{2}$ $+ \ \frac{2}{3}$
4.	$\frac{1}{3}$ $3\frac{2}{3}$ $+ 9\frac{7}{12}$	$2\frac{3}{10}$ $15\frac{3}{5}$ $+ \ \frac{7}{10}$	$1\frac{1}{2}$ $17\frac{1}{2}$ $+ \ \frac{7}{10}$	$2\frac{3}{8}$ $\frac{5}{8}$ $+ 7\frac{1}{2}$

Subtraction of Fractions with Different Denominators

To subtract fractions with different denominators, first rewrite the fractions as equivalent fractions with like denominators. Then subtract and simplify the answer.

Find: $\frac{4}{5} - \frac{3}{4}$

Write equivalent fractions with like denominators. Use the LCD.

$$\frac{4}{5} = \frac{4 \times 4}{5 \times 4} = \frac{16}{20}$$
$$-\frac{3}{4} = \frac{3 \times 5}{4 \times 5} = \frac{15}{20}$$

Subtract the numerators. Use the same denominators.

$$\frac{4}{5} = \frac{16}{20}$$
$$-\frac{3}{4} = \frac{15}{20}$$
$$\overline{\quad \frac{1}{20} \quad}$$

Subtract. Simplify.

	a	b	c	d
1.	$\frac{1}{3} = \frac{4}{12}$ $-\frac{1}{4} = \frac{3}{12}$ $\overline{\quad \frac{1}{12} \quad}$	$\frac{1}{4} = \frac{}{20}$ $-\frac{1}{5} = \frac{}{20}$	$\frac{3}{5} = \frac{}{10}$ $-\frac{1}{2} = \frac{}{10}$	$\frac{2}{3} = \frac{}{6}$ $-\frac{1}{2} = \frac{}{6}$
2.	$\frac{5}{6}$ $-\frac{1}{4}$	$\frac{5}{6}$ $-\frac{3}{8}$	$\frac{4}{5}$ $-\frac{1}{2}$	$\frac{1}{2}$ $-\frac{1}{5}$
3.	$\frac{4}{5}$ $-\frac{3}{10}$	$\frac{5}{6}$ $-\frac{5}{9}$	$\frac{3}{4}$ $-\frac{3}{8}$	$\frac{7}{9}$ $-\frac{1}{4}$

Set up the problems. Then find the differences. Simplify.

a

4. $\frac{14}{15} - \frac{1}{3} = $ _____

$\frac{14}{15}$
$-\frac{1}{3}$
$\overline{\qquad}$

b

$\frac{8}{9} - \frac{3}{8} = $ _____

c

$\frac{11}{12} - \frac{3}{8} = $ _____

Subtraction of Fractions and Mixed Numbers from Whole Numbers

Sometimes you will need to subtract a fraction from a whole number.
Write the whole number as a mixed number with a like denominator.
Subtract the fractions. Subtract the whole numbers.

Find: $7 - 2\frac{5}{8}$

| To subtract, you need two fractions with like denominators.

7
$-2\frac{5}{8}$ | Write 7 as a mixed number with 8 as the denominator.

$7 = 6 + \frac{8}{8} = 6\frac{8}{8}$

Remember, $\frac{8}{8} = 1$ | Subtract the fractions.

$\begin{aligned}7 &= 6\frac{8}{8}\\ -2\frac{5}{8} &= 2\frac{5}{8}\\ \hline &\quad\frac{3}{8}\end{aligned}$ | Subtract the whole numbers.

$\begin{aligned}7 &= 6\frac{8}{8}\\ -2\frac{5}{8} &= 2\frac{5}{8}\\ \hline &\ 4\frac{3}{8}\end{aligned}$ |

Write each whole number as a mixed number.

	a	b	c	d
1.	$8 = 7 + \frac{4}{4} = 7\frac{4}{4}$	$12 = 11 + \frac{3}{\_} =$	$18 = 17 + \frac{\_}{8} =$	$28 = 27 + \frac{12}{\_} =$

Subtract. Simplify.

	a	b	c	d
2.	$\begin{aligned}8 &= 7\frac{3}{3}\\ -4\frac{2}{3} &= 4\frac{2}{3}\\ \hline &\ 3\frac{1}{3}\end{aligned}$	$\begin{aligned}4 &= 3\frac{\_}{4}\\ -2\frac{3}{4} &= 2\frac{3}{4}\\ \hline\end{aligned}$	$\begin{aligned}6 &= 5\frac{\_}{8}\\ -2\frac{5}{8} &= 2\frac{5}{8}\\ \hline\end{aligned}$	$\begin{aligned}14 &= 13\frac{\_}{6}\\ -9\frac{5}{6} &= 9\frac{5}{6}\\ \hline\end{aligned}$
3.	$\begin{aligned}15\ \ \\ -12\frac{1}{2}\\ \hline\end{aligned}$	$\begin{aligned}19\ \ \\ -14\frac{5}{8}\\ \hline\end{aligned}$	$\begin{aligned}12\ \ \\ -8\frac{1}{5}\\ \hline\end{aligned}$	$\begin{aligned}15\ \ \\ -\frac{3}{10}\\ \hline\end{aligned}$
4.	$\begin{aligned}12\ \ \\ -9\frac{1}{6}\\ \hline\end{aligned}$	$\begin{aligned}16\ \ \\ -\frac{3}{4}\\ \hline\end{aligned}$	$\begin{aligned}13\ \ \\ -10\frac{5}{9}\\ \hline\end{aligned}$	$\begin{aligned}9\ \ \\ -\frac{3}{5}\\ \hline\end{aligned}$

Subtraction of Mixed Numbers with Regrouping

To subtract mixed numbers, it may be necessary to regroup first. Write the whole number part as a mixed number. Add the mixed number and the fraction. Then subtract and simplify.

Find: $8\frac{7}{12} - 2\frac{3}{4}$

Write the fractions with like denominators. Compare the numerators.

$8\frac{7}{12} = 8\frac{7}{12}$
$-2\frac{3}{4} = 2\frac{9}{12}$

$\frac{9}{12}$ is greater than $\frac{7}{12}$. You can't subtract the fractions.

To regroup, write **8** as a mixed number.

$8 = 7\frac{12}{12}$

Add the mixed number and the fraction.

$8\frac{7}{12} = 7\frac{12}{12} + \frac{7}{12} = 7\frac{19}{12}$

Remember, $\frac{19}{12}$ is an improper fraction.

Now you can subtract and simplify.

$8\frac{7}{12} = 7\frac{19}{12}$
$-2\frac{9}{12} = 2\frac{9}{12}$
$\phantom{-2\frac{9}{12} = }5\frac{10}{12} = 5\frac{5}{6}$

Subtract. Simplify.

	a	b	c

1.
$8\frac{1}{5} = 7\frac{6}{5}$
$-2\frac{4}{5} = 2\frac{4}{5}$
$\phantom{-2\frac{4}{5} = }5\frac{2}{5}$

$7\frac{1}{4} = 6\frac{}{4}$
$-\frac{3}{4} = \frac{3}{4}$

$8\frac{7}{12} = 7\frac{}{12}$
$-4\frac{11}{12} = 4\frac{11}{12}$

2.
$9\frac{3}{8}$
$-\frac{1}{2}$

$10\frac{1}{3}$
$-8\frac{2}{3}$

$7\frac{1}{5}$
$-4\frac{5}{8}$

3.
$16\frac{1}{12}$
$-9\frac{11}{12}$

$12\frac{1}{10}$
$-\frac{1}{5}$

$16\frac{1}{2}$
$-8\frac{4}{9}$

Set up the problems. Then find the differences. Simplify.

	a	b	c

4. $6\frac{3}{5} - 4\frac{9}{10} = $ _____

$6\frac{3}{5}$
$-4\frac{9}{10}$

$9\frac{1}{4} - 7\frac{3}{7} = $ _____

$15\frac{1}{3} - \frac{2}{3} = $ _____

Problem-Solving Method: Use Estimation

Stacey's bowl holds 15 cups of punch. Her recipe for punch is $9\frac{1}{3}$ cups of juice mixed with $6\frac{3}{4}$ cups of ginger ale. Does she need a bigger bowl?

Understand the problem.

- **What do you want to know?**
  if the punch will fit in the bowl

- **What information is given?**
  The bowl holds 15 cups.
  The punch is made with $9\frac{1}{3}$ cups of juice and $6\frac{3}{4}$ cups of ginger ale.

Plan how to solve it.

- **What method can you use?**
  Since the problem is not asking for an exact answer, you can use estimation to find the sum of the punch ingredients.

Solve it.

- **How can you use this method to solve the problem?**
  Round the mixed numbers to whole numbers. If the fractional part is less than $\frac{1}{2}$, drop the fraction and leave the whole number unchanged. If it is greater than or equal to $\frac{1}{2}$, round up to the next whole number.

$$
\begin{array}{llll}
9\frac{1}{3} & \textbf{Think: } \frac{1}{3} < \frac{1}{2} & \text{Round down.} & 9 \\
+6\frac{3}{4} & \textbf{Think: } \frac{3}{4} > \frac{1}{2} & \text{Round up.} & +\;7 \\
\hline
& & & \textbf{16 cups of punch}
\end{array}
$$

- **What is the answer?**
  Stacey needs a bigger bowl.

Look back and check your answer.

- **Is your answer reasonable?**
  You can check your estimate by finding the exact answer.

$$
\begin{array}{rl}
9\frac{1}{3} = & 9\frac{4}{12} \\
+6\frac{3}{4} = & 6\frac{9}{12} \\
\hline
& 15\frac{13}{12} = 16\frac{1}{12}
\end{array}
$$

The exact answer shows that the 15-cup bowl is not large enough to hold all the punch.
The estimate is reasonable.

Use estimation to solve each problem.

1. Kim leaves her house at 10:00 A.M. It takes $1\frac{1}{2}$ hours to drive to the airport and $\frac{3}{4}$ hour to check in. Will she make her 12:00 PM flight?

Answer _____

2. Tom planned to sell his stock when it reached $25 per share. In the morning, the stock was $19\frac{1}{5}$ per share. It went up $6\frac{2}{9}$ by the afternoon. Did he sell his stock?

Answer _____

3. Maya hiked $15\frac{3}{8}$ miles on Saturday and $13\frac{1}{2}$ miles on Sunday. Her 2-day goal was to hike 30 miles. Did she reach her goal?

Answer _____

4. It snowed $2\frac{1}{4}$ inches on Monday, 3 inches on Tuesday, and $\frac{5}{8}$ inch on Wednesday. About how many inches did it snow in the three days altogether?

Answer _____

5. Ellen has 4 cups of sugar. She needs $3\frac{2}{3}$ cups to make a cake and $1\frac{1}{4}$ cups to make the icing. Does she have enough sugar?

Answer _____

UNIT 2 Review

Write the fraction and the word name for the part that is shaded.

      a   *b*   *c*

1.    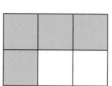   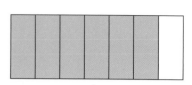

_____ or _____   _____ or _____   _____ or _____

Write as a whole or mixed number. Simplify.

     a   *b*   *c*   *d*

2. $\frac{35}{5} =$ _____ $\frac{26}{3} =$ _____ $\frac{15}{3} =$ _____ $\frac{21}{6} =$ _____

Write as an improper fraction.

     a   *b*   *c*   *d*

3. $3\frac{1}{4} =$ _____ $2\frac{7}{8} =$ _____ $4\frac{3}{5} =$ _____ $1\frac{7}{10} =$ _____

Rewrite each fraction as an equivalent fraction in higher terms.

     a   *b*   *c*   *d*

4. $\frac{4}{7} = \frac{}{21}$ $\frac{1}{9} = \frac{}{45}$ $\frac{2}{3} = \frac{}{24}$ $\frac{5}{6} = \frac{}{18}$

Use the LCD to write equivalent fractions.

     a   *b*   *c*   *d*

5. $\frac{1}{4} =$ $\frac{1}{5} =$ $\frac{3}{8} =$ $\frac{1}{2} =$

      $\frac{1}{3} =$ $\frac{3}{4} =$ $\frac{2}{3} =$ $\frac{4}{11} =$

Simplify.

     a   *b*   *c*   *d*

6. $\frac{4}{24} =$ $\frac{3}{9} =$ $\frac{2}{30} =$ $\frac{15}{45} =$

7. $\frac{6}{42} =$ $\frac{12}{20} =$ $\frac{3}{27} =$ $\frac{16}{32} =$

Add. Simplify.

	a	b	c	d

8.
$\begin{array}{r} \frac{2}{7} \\ + \frac{6}{7} \\ \hline \end{array}$
$\begin{array}{r} \frac{2}{3} \\ + \frac{1}{9} \\ \hline \end{array}$
$\begin{array}{r} 1 \\ + 2\frac{3}{11} \\ \hline \end{array}$
$\begin{array}{r} 3\frac{3}{8} \\ + 2\frac{1}{5} \\ \hline \end{array}$

9.
$\begin{array}{r} 3\frac{8}{9} \\ + 5 \\ \hline \end{array}$
$\begin{array}{r} 2\frac{5}{12} \\ + 4\frac{7}{8} \\ \hline \end{array}$
$\begin{array}{r} 1\frac{9}{10} \\ + 3\frac{4}{5} \\ \hline \end{array}$
$\begin{array}{r} \frac{1}{6} \\ + \frac{2}{7} \\ \hline \end{array}$

10.
$\begin{array}{r} \frac{3}{4} \\ + \frac{5}{6} \\ \hline \end{array}$
$\begin{array}{r} \frac{4}{7} \\ + 15\frac{1}{3} \\ \hline \end{array}$
$\begin{array}{r} \frac{6}{11} \\ + 5\frac{9}{11} \\ \hline \end{array}$
$\begin{array}{r} 4 \\ + \frac{9}{16} \\ \hline \end{array}$

11.
$\begin{array}{r} 1\frac{5}{6} \\ \frac{2}{3} \\ + 4 \\ \hline \end{array}$
$\begin{array}{r} 9\frac{2}{3} \\ \frac{1}{9} \\ + 12 \\ \hline \end{array}$
$\begin{array}{r} \frac{5}{6} \\ 9\frac{1}{4} \\ + 18 \\ \hline \end{array}$
$\begin{array}{r} 6\frac{7}{8} \\ 3\frac{4}{5} \\ + 2 \\ \hline \end{array}$

Subtract. Simplify.

	a	b	c	d

12.
$\begin{array}{r} \frac{5}{8} \\ - \frac{1}{3} \\ \hline \end{array}$
$\begin{array}{r} 8 \\ - 2\frac{2}{5} \\ \hline \end{array}$
$\begin{array}{r} 3 \\ - \frac{3}{7} \\ \hline \end{array}$
$\begin{array}{r} 5\frac{11}{12} \\ - 3\frac{1}{6} \\ \hline \end{array}$

13.
$\begin{array}{r} 4 \\ - 3\frac{1}{2} \\ \hline \end{array}$
$\begin{array}{r} 2 \\ - \frac{11}{12} \\ \hline \end{array}$
$\begin{array}{r} \frac{5}{8} \\ - \frac{3}{8} \\ \hline \end{array}$
$\begin{array}{r} \frac{5}{6} \\ - \frac{1}{4} \\ \hline \end{array}$

14.
$\begin{array}{r} 7\frac{1}{4} \\ - 2\frac{5}{9} \\ \hline \end{array}$
$\begin{array}{r} \frac{4}{5} \\ - \frac{1}{2} \\ \hline \end{array}$
$\begin{array}{r} 9\frac{1}{12} \\ - 2\frac{5}{8} \\ \hline \end{array}$
$\begin{array}{r} 2\frac{1}{4} \\ - \frac{3}{4} \\ \hline \end{array}$

15.
$\begin{array}{r} 10\frac{3}{5} \\ - 8\frac{1}{4} \\ \hline \end{array}$
$\begin{array}{r} 4\frac{1}{7} \\ - \frac{2}{7} \\ \hline \end{array}$
$\begin{array}{r} 5\frac{6}{9} \\ - 1\frac{4}{5} \\ \hline \end{array}$
$\begin{array}{r} \frac{7}{11} \\ - \frac{5}{9} \\ \hline \end{array}$

Unit 3
Multiplication and Division of Fractions

Multiplication of Fractions

To multiply fractions, multiply the numerators and multiply the denominators. Simplify the product.

Find: $\frac{1}{2} \times \frac{3}{4}$

Multiply the numerators.

$\frac{1}{2} \times \frac{3}{4} = \frac{1 \times 3}{} = \frac{3}{}$

Multiply the denominators.

$\frac{1}{2} \times \frac{3}{4} = \frac{1 \times 3}{2 \times 4} = \frac{3}{8}$

Find: $\frac{3}{4} \times \frac{2}{6}$

Multiply the numerators.

$\frac{3}{4} \times \frac{2}{6} = \frac{3 \times 2}{} = \frac{6}{}$

Multiply the denominators. Simplify.

$\frac{3}{4} \times \frac{2}{6} = \frac{3 \times 2}{4 \times 6} = \frac{6}{24} = \frac{1}{4}$

Multiply. Simplify.

	a	*b*
1.	$\frac{2}{5} \times \frac{1}{3} = \frac{2 \times 1}{5 \times 3} = \frac{2}{15}$	$\frac{3}{10} \times \frac{1}{5} =$
2.	$\frac{4}{7} \times \frac{3}{5} =$	$\frac{5}{6} \times \frac{7}{8} =$
3.	$\frac{1}{2} \times \frac{4}{7} =$	$\frac{1}{3} \times \frac{6}{11} =$
4.	$\frac{3}{4} \times \frac{1}{3} =$	$\frac{5}{8} \times \frac{3}{10} =$
5.	$\frac{4}{10} \times \frac{5}{16} =$	$\frac{3}{12} \times \frac{1}{3} =$

Multiplication of Fractions Using Cancellation

Instead of simplifying fractions after they have been multiplied,
it may be possible to use **cancellation** before multiplying.
To cancel, find a common factor of a numerator and a denominator.
Divide the numerator and the denominator by the common
factor. Then multiply, using the new numerator and denominator.

Find: $\frac{3}{4} \times \frac{2}{5}$ using cancellation.

Find the common factor.	Cancel.	Multiply the new numerators and denominators. Simplify.
$\frac{3}{4} \times \frac{2}{5}$	$\frac{3}{\cancel{4}} \times \frac{\cancel{2}^{1}}{5}$ $\quad_{2}$	$\frac{3 \times 1}{2 \times 5} = \frac{3}{10}$
The common factor of 4 and 2 is 2.	Divide both the 4 and the 2 by 2.	

Multiply using cancellation.

a

1. $\frac{3}{4} \times \frac{1}{3} = \frac{\cancel{3}^{1}}{4} \times \frac{1}{\cancel{3}_{1}} = \frac{1 \times 1}{4 \times 1} = \frac{1}{4}$

b

$\frac{7}{8} \times \frac{4}{9} =$

2. $\frac{4}{7} \times \frac{3}{8} =$ $\frac{5}{16} \times \frac{1}{5} =$

3. $\frac{2}{3} \times \frac{1}{8} =$ $\frac{3}{4} \times \frac{1}{9} =$

4. $\frac{7}{10} \times \frac{5}{6} =$ $\frac{3}{4} \times \frac{13}{15} =$

5. $\frac{5}{6} \times \frac{3}{10} =$ $\frac{4}{9} \times \frac{3}{8} =$

6. $\frac{2}{3} \times \frac{3}{4} =$ $\frac{4}{5} \times \frac{5}{8} =$

Multiplication of Whole Numbers by Fractions

To multiply a whole number by a fraction, first write the whole number as an improper fraction. Use cancellation if possible. Multiply the numerators and the denominators. Simplify.

Find: $8 \times \frac{5}{16}$

Write the whole number as an improper fraction.	Cancel.	Multiply using the new numbers. Simplify.
$8 \times \frac{5}{16} = \frac{8}{1} \times \frac{5}{16}$	$\frac{\overset{1}{\cancel{8}}}{1} \times \frac{5}{\underset{2}{\cancel{16}}}$	$\frac{1 \times 5}{1 \times 2} = \frac{5}{2} = 2\frac{1}{2}$
	Divide 8 and 16 by 8.	

Write each whole number as a fraction.

a	b	c	d	e
1. $7 = \frac{7}{1}$	$18 =$	$20 =$	$4 =$	$12 =$

Multiply using cancellation. Simplify.

a	b	c
2. $10 \times \frac{1}{5} = \frac{\overset{2}{\cancel{10}}}{1} \times \frac{1}{\underset{1}{\cancel{5}}} = \frac{2 \times 1}{1 \times 1} = 2$	$14 \times \frac{2}{7} =$	$15 \times \frac{3}{10} =$
3. $9 \times \frac{1}{6} =$	$12 \times \frac{3}{4} =$	$8 \times \frac{5}{6} =$
4. $\frac{2}{3} \times 9 =$	$\frac{3}{10} \times 25 =$	$\frac{4}{5} \times 25 =$
5. $\frac{8}{9} \times 27 =$	$\frac{11}{16} \times 24 =$	$\frac{5}{8} \times 32 =$

Multiplication of Mixed Numbers by Whole Numbers

To multiply a mixed number by a whole number, first write the mixed number and the whole number as improper fractions. Use cancellation if possible. Multiply the new numerators and denominators. Simplify the answer.

Find: $4\frac{1}{2} \times 6$

Write the whole number and the mixed number as improper fractions.	Cancel.	Multiply the new numerators and denominators. Simplify.
$4\frac{1}{2} \times 6 = \frac{9}{2} \times \frac{6}{1}$	$\frac{9}{\underset{1}{2}} \times \frac{\overset{3}{6}}{1}$	$\frac{9 \times 3}{1 \times 1} = \frac{27}{1} = 27$

Multiply. Simplify. Use cancellation if possible.

a	b	c
1. $2\frac{1}{2} \times 6 =$	$2\frac{1}{3} \times 3 =$	$4\frac{1}{2} \times 8 =$
$\frac{5}{\underset{1}{2}} \times \frac{\overset{3}{6}}{1} = \frac{15}{1} = 15$		
2. $4 \times 2\frac{1}{2} =$	$6 \times 2\frac{1}{3} =$	$1\frac{3}{4} \times 8 =$
3. $6 \times 2\frac{1}{6} =$	$9 \times 2\frac{1}{3} =$	$4 \times 12\frac{1}{2} =$
4. $3\frac{1}{3} \times 20 =$	$2 \times 5\frac{3}{4} =$	$4 \times 3\frac{1}{5} =$
5. $4 \times 2\frac{1}{10} =$	$5 \times 2\frac{1}{15} =$	$11 \times 7\frac{4}{22} =$
6. $8\frac{4}{15} \times 5 =$	$4\frac{1}{9} \times 30 =$	$2\frac{4}{9} \times 2 =$

Multiplication of Mixed Numbers by Fractions

To multiply a mixed number by a fraction, first write the mixed number as an improper fraction. Use cancellation if possible. Multiply the new numerators and denominators. Simplify.

Find: $2\frac{1}{4} \times \frac{1}{3}$

Write the mixed number as an improper fraction.	Cancel.	Multiply the new numerators and denominators.
$2\frac{1}{4} \times \frac{1}{3} = \frac{9}{4} \times \frac{1}{3}$	$\frac{\overset{3}{\cancel{9}}}{4} \times \frac{1}{\underset{1}{\cancel{3}}}$	$\frac{3 \times 1}{4 \times 1} = \frac{3}{4}$

Multiply. Simplify. Use cancellation if possible.

	a	b	c
1.	$\frac{2}{5} \times 1\frac{1}{2} =$	$\frac{3}{8} \times 1\frac{3}{5} =$	$\frac{1}{5} \times 4\frac{1}{6} =$
	$\frac{\overset{1}{\cancel{2}}}{5} \times \frac{3}{\underset{1}{\cancel{2}}} = \frac{3}{5}$		
2.	$\frac{7}{8} \times 2\frac{2}{5} =$	$1\frac{1}{4} \times \frac{3}{5} =$	$\frac{7}{10} \times 1\frac{3}{14} =$
3.	$\frac{7}{10} \times 1\frac{1}{3} =$	$\frac{2}{3} \times 5\frac{7}{8} =$	$\frac{4}{5} \times 6\frac{3}{4} =$
4.	$4\frac{1}{2} \times \frac{2}{3} =$	$5\frac{1}{4} \times \frac{2}{3} =$	$8\frac{3}{4} \times \frac{2}{5} =$
5.	$12\frac{1}{2} \times \frac{4}{5} =$	$2\frac{3}{4} \times \frac{4}{22} =$	$3\frac{3}{4} \times \frac{16}{20} =$

Multiplication of Mixed Numbers by Mixed Numbers

To multiply a mixed number by a mixed number, write both mixed numbers as improper fractions. Use cancellation if possible. Then multiply the new numerators and denominators. Simplify.

Find: $3\frac{2}{3} \times 4\frac{1}{2}$

Write the mixed numbers as improper fractions.	Cancel.	Multiply the new numerators and denominators. Simplify.
$3\frac{2}{3} \times 4\frac{1}{2} = \frac{11}{3} \times \frac{9}{2}$	$\frac{11}{\overset{}{\underset{1}{3}}} \times \frac{\overset{3}{9}}{2}$	$\frac{11 \times 3}{1 \times 2} = \frac{33}{2} = 16\frac{1}{2}$

Multiply. Simplify. Use cancellation if possible.

	a	b	c
1.	$3\frac{1}{5} \times 2\frac{1}{4} =$	$1\frac{1}{2} \times 1\frac{1}{2} =$	$1\frac{2}{3} \times 1\frac{3}{5} =$
	$\frac{\overset{4}{16}}{5} \times \frac{9}{\underset{1}{4}} = \frac{36}{5} = 7\frac{1}{5}$		
2.	$2\frac{1}{2} \times 3\frac{1}{3} =$	$4\frac{1}{3} \times 3\frac{3}{4} =$	$2\frac{3}{4} \times 2\frac{2}{3} =$
3.	$5\frac{1}{4} \times 3\frac{1}{2} =$	$4\frac{1}{2} \times 3\frac{1}{5} =$	$6\frac{3}{4} \times 8\frac{1}{3} =$
4.	$4\frac{4}{5} \times 3\frac{1}{8} =$	$4\frac{2}{7} \times 2\frac{1}{10} =$	$5\frac{5}{8} \times 2\frac{2}{3} =$
5.	$3\frac{3}{5} \times 3\frac{1}{3} =$	$2\frac{4}{10} \times 3\frac{1}{3} =$	$4\frac{4}{5} \times 1\frac{7}{8} =$

Problem-Solving Method: Solve Multi-step Problems

Babies gain an average of $2\frac{1}{5}$ pounds each month for the first three months after they are born. Matt weighs $7\frac{1}{2}$ pounds at birth. How much will he probably weigh in 3 months?

Understand the problem.

- **What do you want to know?**
  Matt's weight after 3 months

- **What information is given?**
  He weighs $7\frac{1}{2}$ pounds at birth.
  He gains about $2\frac{1}{5}$ pounds each of the 3 months.

Plan how to solve it.

- **What method can you use?**
  You can separate the problem into steps.

Solve it.

- **How can you use this method to solve the problem?**
  First find the total weight Matt will gain in the 3 months.
  Then add that total to his birth weight.

Step 1	Step 2
$2\frac{1}{5} \times 3 = \frac{11}{5} \times \frac{3}{1} = \frac{33}{5} = 6\frac{3}{5}$ **Total weight gain = $6\frac{3}{5}$ pounds**	$\begin{aligned} 7\frac{1}{2} &= 7\frac{5}{10} \\ + 6\frac{3}{5} &= 6\frac{6}{10} \\ \hline &= 13\frac{11}{10} = 14\frac{1}{10} \text{ pounds} \end{aligned}$

- **What is the answer?**
  Matt will probably weigh $14\frac{1}{10}$ pounds in 3 months.

Look back and check your answer.

- **Is your answer reasonable?**
  You can add to check your multiplication.

$$7\frac{1}{2} + 2\frac{1}{5} + 2\frac{1}{5} + 2\frac{1}{5} = 14\frac{1}{10}$$

The answer matches the sum.
The answer is reasonable.

Separate each problem into steps to solve.

1. On average, a baby's head grows $\frac{1}{2}$ inch every month for the first 4 months after birth. Then, from 4 months old to 1 year old, it grows another 2 inches. How many inches does a baby's head grow the first year after it is born?
(1 year = 12 months)

Answer _____

2. Mei earns $8 an hour at the coffee shop. She worked $7\frac{1}{2}$ hours on Saturday and $5\frac{1}{4}$ hours on Sunday. How much money did she earn for the 2 days altogether?

Answer _____

3. The average person dreams for $\frac{1}{4}$ of the time he or she sleeps. If Anna sleeps for 8 hours, and Brian sleeps for 9 hours, how much longer does Brian dream?

Answer _____

4. Antoine mixed $1\frac{1}{4}$ gallons of blue paint with $\frac{4}{5}$ gallon of yellow paint to make green. Then he mixed $1\frac{3}{4}$ gallons of red paint with $\frac{1}{2}$ gallon of white paint to make pink. Which color did Antoine mix the most of, green or pink?

Answer _____

5. United States athletes set some top records for long jumps. The third longest was $29\frac{1}{12}$ feet. The second longest was $\frac{2}{3}$ foot longer than the third. The world's longest jump was $\frac{2}{3}$ foot longer than the second. Which of these jumps was the longest?

Answer _____

6. A recipe for 1 batch of sugar cookies needs $\frac{3}{4}$ tablespoon of vanilla. One batch of lemon cookies needs $\frac{1}{2}$ tablespoon of vanilla. If Ken makes 2 batches of sugar cookies and $\frac{1}{2}$ a batch of lemon cookies, how much vanilla does he need in all?

Answer _____

Finding Reciprocals

To divide by a fraction, you need to know how to find reciprocals.
Reciprocals are numbers whose numerators and denominators have been inverted, or switched. The product of two reciprocals is 1.

Write the reciprocals.

| $\frac{3}{4}$ reciprocal $= \frac{4}{3}$ | $\frac{1}{5}$ reciprocal $= \frac{5}{1} = 5$ | $7 = \frac{7}{1}$ reciprocal $= \frac{1}{7}$ |

Write the reciprocal.

	a	b	c	d	e
1.	$\frac{2}{3}$ ___ $\frac{3}{2}$	$\frac{1}{6}$ ___	$\frac{7}{8}$ ___	$\frac{5}{9}$ ___	8 ___
2.	$\frac{3}{5}$ ___	$\frac{9}{13}$ ___	$\frac{7}{4}$ ___	25 ___	$\frac{1}{4}$ ___

Write as an improper fraction. Then write the reciprocal.

	a	b	c	d
3.	$4\frac{1}{3} =$ ___ $\frac{13}{3}$ $\frac{3}{13}$	$2\frac{4}{5}$ ___	$1\frac{7}{9}$ ___	$5\frac{1}{4}$ ___
4.	$5\frac{1}{11}$ ___	$1\frac{8}{13}$ ___	$6\frac{1}{8}$ ___	$3\frac{5}{6}$ ___

Write the missing factor.

	a	b	c	d
5.	$\frac{7}{9} \times$ $\frac{9}{7}$ $= 1$	$\frac{1}{5} \times$ ___ $= 1$	$9 \times$ ___ $= 1$	$3\frac{1}{2} \times$ ___ $= 1$

Division of Fractions by Fractions

To divide a fraction by a fraction, multiply by the reciprocal of the second fraction. Simplify the answer if needed. Remember, only the second fraction is inverted.

Find: $\frac{5}{8} \div \frac{3}{4}$

Multiply by the reciprocal of the second fraction.	Cancel.	Multiply the new numerators and denominators.
$\frac{5}{8} \div \frac{3}{4} = \frac{5}{8} \times \frac{4}{3}$	$\frac{5}{\overset{}{\underset{2}{8}}} \times \frac{\overset{1}{4}}{3}$	$\frac{5 \times 1}{2 \times 3} = \frac{5}{6}$

Divide. Simplify.

              a   *b*

1. $\frac{2}{3} \div \frac{5}{7} = \frac{2}{3} \times \frac{7}{5} = \frac{2 \times 7}{3 \times 5} = \frac{14}{15}$ $\frac{3}{8} \div \frac{1}{3} = \frac{3}{8} \times \frac{3}{1} = \frac{3 \times 3}{8 \times 1} =$

2. $\frac{8}{15} \div \frac{16}{45} = \frac{8}{15} \times \qquad =$ $\frac{9}{16} \div \frac{3}{8} = \frac{9}{16} \times \qquad =$

         a   *b*   *c*

3. $\frac{4}{5} \div \frac{1}{10} =$ $\frac{5}{12} \div \frac{3}{4} =$ $\frac{1}{5} \div \frac{1}{20} =$

4. $\frac{1}{4} \div \frac{4}{9} =$ $\frac{5}{8} \div \frac{5}{8} =$ $\frac{5}{12} \div \frac{3}{2} =$

5. $\frac{3}{10} \div \frac{1}{10} =$ $\frac{7}{12} \div \frac{3}{8} =$ $\frac{11}{32} \div \frac{5}{16} =$

6. $\frac{15}{16} \div \frac{3}{5} =$ $\frac{17}{18} \div \frac{2}{3} =$ $\frac{11}{12} \div \frac{1}{6} =$

Division of Fractions by Whole Numbers

To divide a fraction by a whole number, multiply by the reciprocal of the whole number. Simplify the quotient. Remember, the reciprocal of a whole number is 1 divided by that number.

Find: $\frac{3}{4} \div 12$

Multiply by the reciprocal of the whole number.	Cancel.	Multiply.
$\frac{3}{4} \times \frac{1}{12}$	$\frac{\overset{1}{\cancel{3}}}{4} \times \frac{1}{\underset{4}{\cancel{12}}}$	$\frac{1 \times 1}{4 \times 4} = \frac{1}{16}$

Divide. Simplify.

1. $\frac{5}{8} \div 10 = \frac{\overset{1}{\cancel{5}}}{8} \times \frac{1}{\underset{2}{\cancel{10}}} = \frac{1 \times 1}{8 \times 2} = \frac{1}{16}$ *a*

b $\frac{3}{4} \div 6 = \frac{3}{4} \times \frac{1}{6} =$

2. $\frac{3}{4} \div 2 = \frac{3}{4} \times \qquad =$ $\frac{7}{15} \div 7 = \frac{7}{15} \times \qquad =$

           a   *b*   *c*

3. $\frac{6}{7} \div 18 =$ $\frac{7}{10} \div 21 =$ $\frac{5}{12} \div 20 =$

4. $\frac{7}{8} \div 28 =$ $\frac{5}{6} \div 30 =$ $\frac{8}{15} \div 16 =$

5. $\frac{15}{16} \div 5 =$ $\frac{2}{15} \div 8 =$ $\frac{4}{13} \div 20 =$

6. $\frac{7}{10} \div 35 =$ $\frac{11}{12} \div 33 =$ $\frac{21}{25} \div 14 =$

Division of Whole Numbers by Fractions

To divide a whole number by a fraction, write the whole number as an improper fraction. Multiply by the reciprocal of the second fraction. Simplify the answer.

Find: $12 \div \frac{3}{4}$

Write the whole number as an improper fraction.	Multiply by the reciprocal of the second fraction.	Cancel.	Multiply and simplify.
$12 \div \frac{3}{4} = \frac{12}{1} \div \frac{3}{4}$	$\frac{12}{1} \times \frac{4}{3}$	$\frac{\overset{4}{\cancel{12}}}{1} \times \frac{4}{\underset{1}{\cancel{3}}}$	$\frac{4 \times 4}{1 \times 1} = \frac{16}{1} = 16$

Divide. Simplify.

    a

1. $10 \div \frac{4}{5} = \frac{10}{1} \div \frac{4}{5} = \frac{10}{1} \times \frac{\overset{5}{\cancel{5}}}{\underset{2}{\cancel{4}}} = \frac{25}{2} = 12\frac{1}{2}$

2. $3 \div \frac{3}{4} =$

3. $4 \div \frac{2}{7} =$

4. $3 \div \frac{15}{16} =$

5. $4 \div \frac{1}{2} =$

6. $14 \div \frac{3}{7} =$

    b

$5 \div \frac{2}{3} =$

$3 \div \frac{6}{7} =$

$6 \div \frac{2}{5} =$

$27 \div \frac{9}{10} =$

$2 \div \frac{2}{9} =$

$8 \div \frac{2}{3} =$

Division of Mixed Numbers by Whole Numbers

To divide a mixed number by a whole number, write the mixed number as an improper fraction. Multiply by the reciprocal of the whole number. Simplify the answer.

Find: $2\frac{1}{3} \div 7$

Write the mixed number as an improper fraction.	Multiply by the reciprocal of the whole number.	Cancel.	Multiply and simplify.
$2\frac{1}{3} \div 7 = \frac{7}{3} \div \frac{7}{1}$	$\frac{7}{3} \times \frac{1}{7}$	$\frac{\overset{1}{\cancel{7}}}{3} \times \frac{1}{\underset{1}{\cancel{7}}}$	$\frac{1 \times 1}{3 \times 1} = \frac{1}{3}$

Divide. Simplify.

	a	b	c
1.	$3\frac{1}{3} \div 5 =$	$2\frac{1}{2} \div 5 =$	$7\frac{1}{2} \div 3 =$

$\frac{10}{3} \div \frac{5}{1} = \frac{\overset{2}{\cancel{10}}}{3} \times \frac{1}{\underset{1}{\cancel{5}}} = \frac{2}{3}$

2.	$6\frac{2}{3} \div 10 =$	$4\frac{1}{5} \div 3 =$	$5\frac{1}{4} \div 7 =$
3.	$6\frac{2}{3} \div 5 =$	$4\frac{1}{6} \div 10 =$	$1\frac{7}{8} \div 5 =$
4.	$7\frac{1}{5} \div 6 =$	$2\frac{1}{12} \div 15 =$	$8\frac{2}{3} \div 39 =$
5.	$3\frac{4}{7} \div 10 =$	$4\frac{1}{8} \div 11 =$	$5\frac{1}{3} \div 24 =$

Division of Mixed Numbers by Fractions

To divide a mixed number by a fraction, write the mixed number as an improper fraction. Multiply by the reciprocal of the second fraction. Simplify the answer.

Find: $1\frac{3}{4} \div \frac{3}{8}$

Write the mixed number as an improper fraction.	Multiply by the reciprocal of the second fraction.	Cancel.	Multiply and simplify.
$1\frac{3}{4} \div \frac{3}{8} = \frac{7}{4} \div \frac{3}{8}$	$\frac{7}{4} \times \frac{8}{3}$	$\frac{7}{\cancel{4}_1} \times \frac{\cancel{8}^2}{3}$	$\frac{7 \times 2}{1 \times 3} = \frac{14}{3} = 4\frac{2}{3}$

Divide. Simplify.

        a   *b*   *c*

1. $2\frac{1}{3} \div \frac{1}{3} =$ $4\frac{1}{2} \div \frac{1}{2} =$ $3\frac{1}{9} \div \frac{2}{9} =$

$\frac{7}{3} \div \frac{1}{3} = \frac{7}{\cancel{3}_1} \times \frac{\cancel{3}^1}{1} = \frac{7}{1} = 7$

2. $6\frac{5}{8} \div \frac{3}{4} =$ $3\frac{5}{8} \div \frac{1}{4} =$ $1\frac{7}{12} \div \frac{5}{6} =$

3. $5\frac{3}{4} \div \frac{1}{8} =$ $10\frac{4}{5} \div \frac{7}{10} =$ $2\frac{3}{8} \div \frac{19}{21} =$

4. $3\frac{1}{7} \div \frac{4}{11} =$ $2\frac{3}{10} \div \frac{4}{5} =$ $5\frac{1}{7} \div \frac{5}{14} =$

5. $2\frac{3}{4} \div \frac{8}{9} =$ $4\frac{7}{8} \div \frac{7}{8} =$ $4\frac{3}{5} \div \frac{7}{10} =$

Division of Mixed Numbers by Mixed Numbers

To divide a mixed number by a mixed number, write both mixed numbers as improper fractions. Multiply by the reciprocal of the second fraction. Simplify the answer.

Find: $4\frac{3}{4} \div 1\frac{1}{8}$

Write the mixed numbers as improper fractions.	Multiply by the reciprocal of the second fraction.	Cancel.	Multiply and simplify.
$4\frac{3}{4} \div 1\frac{1}{8} = \frac{19}{4} \div \frac{9}{8}$	$\frac{19}{4} \times \frac{8}{9}$	$\frac{19}{\cancel{4}_1} \times \frac{\cancel{8}^2}{9}$	$\frac{19 \times 2}{1 \times 9} = \frac{38}{9} = 4\frac{2}{9}$

Divide. Simplify.

$$a \qquad\qquad\qquad\qquad\qquad\qquad b$$

1. $4\frac{2}{3} \div 3\frac{1}{2} = \frac{14}{3} \div \frac{7}{2} = \frac{\cancel{14}^2}{3} \times \frac{2}{\cancel{7}_1} = \frac{4}{3} = 1\frac{1}{3}$ $\qquad\qquad 16\frac{2}{3} \div 2\frac{1}{2} =$

2. $6\frac{2}{3} \div 6\frac{1}{4} =$ $\qquad\qquad\qquad\qquad\qquad 6\frac{2}{3} \div 1\frac{1}{4} =$

3. $6\frac{2}{5} \div 5\frac{1}{3} =$ $\qquad\qquad\qquad\qquad\qquad 1\frac{1}{5} \div 2\frac{1}{6} =$

4. $6\frac{2}{3} \div 2\frac{1}{8} =$ $\qquad\qquad\qquad\qquad\qquad 3\frac{1}{10} \div 10\frac{1}{3} =$

5. $2\frac{1}{4} \div 3\frac{3}{8} =$ $\qquad\qquad\qquad\qquad\qquad 2\frac{4}{5} \div 1\frac{2}{5} =$

6. $4\frac{2}{3} \div 5\frac{3}{5} =$ $\qquad\qquad\qquad\qquad\qquad 1\frac{1}{9} \div 2\frac{2}{3} =$

Problem-Solving Method: Write a Number Sentence

Some people measure the height of a horse in hands. One inch equals $\frac{1}{4}$ hand. An average Clydesdale horse is 16 hands high. How tall is a Clydesdale in inches?

Understand the problem.

- **What do you want to know?**
  the height of a Clydesdale in inches

- **What information is given?**
  An average Clydesdale horse is 16 hands high.
  1 inch $= \frac{1}{4}$ hand

Plan how to solve it.

- **What method can you use?**
  You can write a number sentence to model the problem.

- **How can you use this method to solve the problem?**
  You want to know how many groups of $\frac{1}{4}$ hand can be divided into the total 16 hands. Write a division number sentence.

$$16 \quad\div\quad \frac{1}{4} \quad=\quad \underline{\hspace{2cm}}$$

| total height in hands | number of hands in 1 inch | total height in inches |

- **What is the answer?**

  $16 \div \frac{1}{4} = \frac{16}{1} \times \frac{4}{1} = 64$

  An average Clydesdale horse is 64 inches tall.

Look back and check your answer.

- **Is your answer reasonable?**
  You can check division with multiplication.

  64 inches $\times \frac{1}{4} = \frac{64}{1} \times \frac{1}{4} = \frac{64}{4} = 16$ hands

  The product matches the dividend.
  The answer is reasonable.

Write a number sentence to solve each problem.

1. Sam had $1\frac{3}{16}$ yards of ribbon. He cut it into pieces $\frac{1}{8}$ of a yard long. How many pieces did he cut?

Answer _____

2. Fresh apples float because $\frac{1}{4}$ of their weight is air. If a bag of apples weighs $2\frac{1}{2}$ pounds, how many pounds is air?

Answer _____

3. During its lifetime, one honeybee makes $\frac{1}{12}$ teaspoon of honey. How many honeybees are needed to make $\frac{1}{2}$ teaspoon of honey?

Answer _____

4. Cheryl has 30 pounds of clay. Each of the refrigerator magnets she is making uses $\frac{3}{4}$ pound of clay. How many magnets can she make?

Answer _____

5. Yuma, Arizona, and Las Vegas, Nevada, are the two driest cities in the United States. Yuma gets an average of $2\frac{2}{3}$ inches of rain each year. Las Vegas gets about $4\frac{1}{5}$ inches. How many inches does it rain each year in the two cities combined?

Answer _____

6. The world's tallest dog was a Great Dane that was $3\frac{5}{11}$ feet tall. The world's smallest dog was a Yorkshire terrier. It was only $\frac{2}{9}$ foot tall. What was the difference between the heights of the two dogs?

Answer _____

Write each whole number as a fraction.

	a	b	c	d	e
1.	$19 =$	$3 =$	$25 =$	$16 =$	$17 =$

Multiply. Use cancellation if possible. Simplify.

	a	b	c
2.	$\frac{2}{5} \times \frac{2}{3} =$	$\frac{2}{3} \times \frac{1}{7} =$	$\frac{1}{2} \times \frac{5}{8} =$
3.	$\frac{1}{2} \times \frac{3}{4} =$	$\frac{5}{6} \times \frac{3}{4} =$	$\frac{2}{8} \times \frac{1}{4} =$
4.	$\frac{15}{16} \times 4 =$	$12 \times \frac{3}{4} =$	$\frac{1}{6} \times 26 =$
5.	$20 \times \frac{2}{5} =$	$24 \times \frac{7}{10} =$	$\frac{2}{3} \times 15 =$
6.	$3\frac{1}{3} \times 4 =$	$9 \times 4\frac{2}{3} =$	$10\frac{1}{5} \times 4 =$
7.	$6\frac{1}{4} \times \frac{3}{5} =$	$\frac{3}{8} \times 4\frac{4}{5} =$	$\frac{1}{6} \times 2\frac{3}{8} =$
8.	$5\frac{1}{3} \times 3\frac{3}{8} =$	$4\frac{3}{5} \times 2\frac{3}{7} =$	$1\frac{1}{2} \times 8\frac{3}{4} =$
9.	$1\frac{4}{7} \times 4\frac{1}{2} =$	$3\frac{2}{3} \times 3\frac{1}{5} =$	$4\frac{1}{4} \times 6\frac{2}{3} =$

Write the reciprocal.

	a	b	c	d	e

10. $\frac{1}{7}$ _____ $\frac{5}{12}$ _____ $\frac{4}{9}$ _____ $2\frac{3}{7}$ _____ $\frac{2}{15}$ _____

Divide. Use cancellation if possible. Simplify.

      a   b   c

11. $\frac{1}{4} \div \frac{1}{8} =$ $\frac{3}{5} \div \frac{1}{5} =$ $\frac{3}{10} \div \frac{2}{7} =$

12. $\frac{2}{3} \div \frac{3}{7} =$ $\frac{1}{9} \div \frac{4}{5} =$ $\frac{4}{11} \div \frac{1}{8} =$

13. $\frac{13}{24} \div 6 =$ $\frac{5}{9} \div 18 =$ $\frac{6}{15} \div 5 =$

14. $\frac{3}{4} \div 12 =$ $\frac{3}{25} \div 9 =$ $\frac{5}{6} \div 10 =$

15. $15 \div \frac{3}{7} =$ $2 \div \frac{1}{12} =$ $7 \div \frac{4}{11} =$

16. $7\frac{1}{5} \div 15 =$ $5\frac{3}{4} \div 12 =$ $2\frac{7}{8} \div 20 =$

17. $12\frac{1}{2} \div 2\frac{3}{4} =$ $6\frac{2}{5} \div 5\frac{1}{3} =$ $4\frac{5}{6} \div 3\frac{4}{7} =$

18. $2\frac{1}{9} \div 7\frac{3}{8} =$ $8\frac{1}{3} \div 1\frac{3}{5} =$ $9\frac{4}{6} \div 3\frac{3}{9} =$

Separate each problem into steps to solve.

19. Sara made hot chocolate mix to give to her neighbors. She mixed $4\frac{1}{4}$ cups of sugar with $2\frac{1}{4}$ cups of cocoa. Then she poured $1\frac{1}{2}$ cups of the mix in each jar. How many jars did she fill?

Answer _____

20. The eucalyptus is the world's fastest growing tree. It grows an average of $2\frac{1}{2}$ centimeters every day. If a eucalyptus tree is 50 centimeters tall when it is planted, how tall will it be in 5 days?

Answer _____

Write a number sentence to solve each problem.

21. Maya runs $3\frac{1}{2}$ miles around the track every morning. One lap around the track is $\frac{1}{8}$ mile. How many times does she run around the track every morning?

Answer _____

22. In the frog-jumping contest, the winner jumped $10\frac{4}{5}$ feet. The second-placed frog jumped $9\frac{3}{4}$ feet. What was the difference in the length of their jumps?

Answer _____

23. Will completed $\frac{1}{3}$ of his passes during the football season. If he threw 90 passes, how many did he complete?

Answer _____

Reading and Writing Decimals

To read a **decimal**, read it as a whole number.
Then name the place value of the last digit.

Read and write 0.246 as two hundred forty-six thousandths.

To read a decimal that has a whole number part,
- read the whole number part.
- read the **decimal point** as *and*.
- read the decimal part as a whole number then name the place value of the last digit.

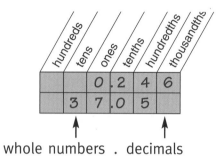

whole numbers . decimals

Read and write 37.05 as thirty-seven and five hundredths.

Write as a decimal.

a   *b*

1. two tenths ___0.2___   two hundredths _____

2. two thousandths _____   six and two hundredths _____

3. twenty-one thousandths _____   one and one thousandths _____

Write each decimal in words.

4. 8.07 ___*eight and seven hundredths*_____

5. 53.009 _____

6. 76.12 _____

Write each money amount with a dollar sign and a decimal point.

a   *b*   *c*

7. six dollars ___$6.00___   sixty cents _____   six cents _____

8. ninety-nine cents _____   twelve cents _____   thirty-one dollars _____

9. four hundred twenty dollars and five cents _____

10. three thousand dollars and ninety-eight cents _____

Comparing and Ordering Decimals

To compare two decimal numbers, begin at the left.
Compare the digits in each place.

The symbol > means **is greater than.** $0.54 > $0.37

The symbol < means **is less than.**   0.829 < 0.84

The symbol = means **is equal to.**   0.23 = 0.230

Compare: 4.1 and 4.3

```
(4).(1)   The ones digits
(4).(3)   are the same.
          Compare
          the tenths.

1 < 3, so 4.1 < 4.3
```

Compare: $0.52 and $0.09

```
$(0).(5) 2   The ones
$(0).(0) 9   digits are
             the same.
             Compare
             the tenths.

5 > 0, so $0.52 > $0.09
```

Compare: 7.5 and 7.52

```
(7).(5)(0)   The ones and
(7).(5)(2)   tenths digits
             are the same.
             Write a zero.
             Compare the
             hundredths.

0 < 2, so 7.5 < 7.52
```

Compare. Write <, >, or =. Write in zeros as needed.

	a	b	c
1.	0.6 __<__ 0.8	0.4 _____ 0.44	0.061 _____ 0.16

	a	b	c
2.	$5.25 _____ $5.50	$4.99 _____ $4.98	$0.83 _____ $0.65
3.	8.9 _____ 8.90	1.36 _____ 1.365	0.921 _____ 0.29

Write in order from least to greatest.

	a	b
4.	0.42 0.4 0.2 _0.2 0.4 0.42_	0.31 0.13 0.031 _____

```
0 . 4 2
0 . 4
0 . 2
```

	a	b
5.	8.1 0.081 0.18 _____	275 2.75 27.5 _____

Fraction and Decimal Equivalents

Sometimes you will need to either change a decimal to a fraction or a fraction to a decimal.

To write a decimal as a fraction, identify the value of the last place in the decimal. Use this place value to write the denominator.

Decimal		Fraction or Mixed Number
0.3	=	$\frac{3}{10}$
0.05	=	$\frac{5}{100}$
0.036	=	$\frac{36}{1,000}$
1.98	=	$\frac{198}{100}$ or $1\frac{98}{100}$

To write a fraction that has a denominator of 10, 100, or 1,000 as a decimal, write the digits from the numerator. Then write the decimal point.

Fraction or Mixed Number		Decimal
$\frac{7}{10}$	=	0.7
$\frac{82}{100}$	=	0.82
$\frac{125}{1,000}$	=	0.125
$\frac{805}{100}$ or $8\frac{05}{100}$	=	8.05

Write each decimal as a fraction.

	a	b	c	d
1.	0.5 $\frac{5}{10}$	0.4 _____	0.2 _____	0.6 _____
2.	0.05 _____	0.04 _____	0.02 _____	0.06 _____

Write each decimal as a mixed number.

	a	b	c	d
3.	2.1 $2\frac{1}{10}$	45.9 _____	31.6 _____	99.9 _____
4.	3.94 _____	6.25 _____	12.54 _____	10.01 _____

Write each fraction as a decimal.

	a	b	c	d
5.	$\frac{9}{10}$ _0.9_	$\frac{3}{10}$ _____	$\frac{1}{10}$ _____	$\frac{8}{10}$ _____
6.	$\frac{7}{100}$ _____	$\frac{91}{100}$ _____	$\frac{63}{1,000}$ _____	$\frac{527}{1,000}$ _____
7.	$\frac{67}{10}$ _____	$\frac{42}{10}$ _____	$\frac{87}{10}$ _____	$\frac{76}{10}$ _____
8.	$\frac{204}{100}$ _____	$\frac{610}{100}$ _____	$\frac{1,754}{1,000}$ _____	$\frac{3,062}{1,000}$ _____

Fraction and Decimal Equivalents

Not all fractions can be changed to **decimal form** easily. To write fractions that have denominators other than 10, 100, or 1,000 as decimals, first write an equivalent fraction that has a denominator of 10, 100, or 1,000. Then write the equivalent fraction as a decimal.

Remember, not all fractions have simple decimal equivalents.

Examples: $\frac{2}{11} = 0.1818\ldots$ and $\frac{2}{3} = 0.666\ldots$

Write $\frac{3}{4}$ as a decimal.

Write $\frac{3}{4}$ with 100 as the denominator.	Write the fraction as a decimal.
$\frac{3}{4} = \frac{3 \times 25}{4 \times 25} = \frac{75}{100}$	$= 0.75$

Write $2\frac{1}{2}$ as a decimal.

Write $2\frac{1}{2}$ as an improper fraction.	Write the new fraction with 10 as the denominator.	Write the fraction as a decimal.
$2\frac{1}{2} = \frac{5}{2}$	$\frac{5}{2} = \frac{5 \times 5}{2 \times 5} = \frac{25}{10}$	$= 2.5$

Write each fraction as a decimal.

	a	b	c
1.	$\frac{2}{5} = \dfrac{2 \times 2}{5 \times 2} = \frac{4}{10} = 0.4$	$\frac{1}{4} =$	$\frac{1}{2} =$
2.	$\frac{5}{20} =$	$\frac{5}{25} =$	$\frac{7}{20} =$
3.	$\frac{17}{4} =$	$\frac{7}{2} =$	$\frac{13}{5} =$
4.	$\frac{37}{25} =$	$\frac{43}{20} =$	$\frac{79}{25} =$

Write each mixed number as a decimal.

	a	b
5.	$6\frac{1}{5} = \dfrac{31}{5} = \dfrac{31 \times 2}{5 \times 2} = \frac{62}{10} = 6.2$	$10\frac{3}{4} =$
6.	$3\frac{5}{25} =$	$4\frac{7}{25} =$
7.	$13\frac{1}{2} =$	$7\frac{2}{5} =$

Problem-Solving Method: Use Logic

Christine Arron, Florence Griffith-Joyner, and Marion Jones are three of the fastest-running women on Earth. Their times for the 100-meter dash are 10.73 seconds, $10\frac{13}{20}$ seconds, and 10.49 seconds. Jones' time has a 6 in the tenths place. Griffith-Joyner is faster than Arron. Who is the fastest-running woman on Earth?

Understand the problem.

- **What do you want to know?**
  who the fastest-running woman on Earth is

- **What information do you know?**
  Their times are 10.73 seconds, $10\frac{13}{20}$ seconds, and 10.49 seconds.
  The fastest time is the smallest number.
  Clue 1: Jones' time has a 6 in the tenths place.
  Clue 2: Griffith-Joyner is faster than Arron.

Plan how to solve it.

- **What method can you use?**
  You can organize all the possibilities in a table.
  Then you can use logic to match the clues to the possibilities.

Solve it.

- **How can you use this method to solve the problem?**
  First, change all the times to decimals so they can be compared.
  Since each of the runners has one time, there can only be one **YES** in each row and column.

	10.73	$10\frac{13}{20} = 10.65$	10.49
Arron	**YES**	no	no
Griffith-Joyner	no	no	**YES**
Jones	no	**YES**	no

- **What is the answer?**
  Florence Griffith-Joyner is the fastest-running woman on Earth.

Look back and check your answer.

- **Is your answer reasonable?**
  Clue 1: Jones' time has a 6 in the tenths place.
  Clue 2: Griffith-Joyner is faster than Arron.

  Check:
  10.**6**5
  $10.49 < 10.73$

  The answer matches the clues.
  The answer is reasonable.

Use logic to solve each problem.

1. Three of the largest earthquakes ever recorded took place in Chile, Russia, and Alaska. They measured $9\frac{1}{10}$, 9.5, and $9\frac{1}{5}$ on the Richter scale. The largest earthquake was in Chile. The earthquake in Russia was smaller than the one in Alaska. What did the three earthquakes measure on the Richter scale?

Chile _____

Russia _____

Alaska _____

2. The National Park Service has measured the Statue of Liberty's hand, face, and the tablet she holds. Their lengths are 16.42 feet, $17\frac{1}{4}$ feet, and 25.58 feet. Her hand is the shortest of the three. The length of her face has a 5 in the hundredths place. What are the lengths of the Statue of Liberty's hand, face, and tablet?

hand _____

face _____

tablet _____

3. Alpha Centauri, Barnard's Star, and Proxima Centauri are the three closest stars to Earth. Their distances from Earth are 5.98 light years, $4\frac{7}{20}$ light years, and $4\frac{11}{50}$ light years. Barnard's Star is farthest from Earth. Alpha Centauri's distance from Earth has a 3 in the tenths place. What is the closest star to Earth?

Answer_____

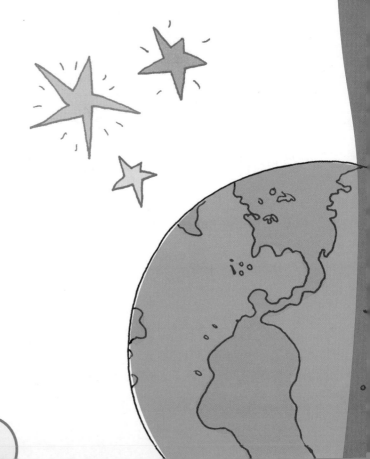

Rounding Decimals

Round decimals to estimate how many. You can use a number line to round decimals.

Remember, when a number is halfway, always round up.

Round 31.2 to the nearest one.

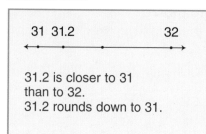

31.2 is closer to 31 than to 32.
31.2 rounds down to 31.

Round $4.67 to the nearest dollar.

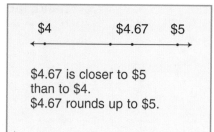

$4.67 is closer to $5 than to $4.
$4.67 rounds up to $5.

Round 6.15 to the nearest tenth.

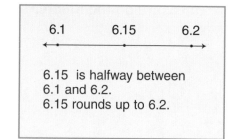

6.15 is halfway between 6.1 and 6.2.
6.15 rounds up to 6.2.

Round to the nearest one.

	a	b	c	d
1.	4.4 _____4_____	3.6 _____	2.5 _____	8.4 _____
2.	43.7 _____	51.5 _____	44.6 _____	73.1 _____
3.	6.39 _____	8.76 _____	5.02 _____	9.93 _____

Round each amount to the nearest dollar.

	a	b	c	d
4.	$3.92 _____$4_____	$25.47 _____	$7.92 _____	$6.35 _____
5.	$8.04 _____	$2.56 _____	$9.53 _____	$62.06 _____
6.	$1.21 _____	$6.49 _____	$2.95 _____	$8.50 _____

Round to the nearest tenth.

	a	b	c	d
7.	0.58 _____0.6_____	0.91 _____	0.64 _____	0.79 _____
8.	4.08 _____	8.67 _____	2.34 _____	9.33 _____
9.	39.96 _____	25.81 _____	72.02 _____	21.63 _____

Addition and Subtraction of Decimals

To add or subtract decimals, line up the decimal points.
Write zeros as needed. Then add or subtract the same way
as whole numbers.

Find: 8.3 + 5.96

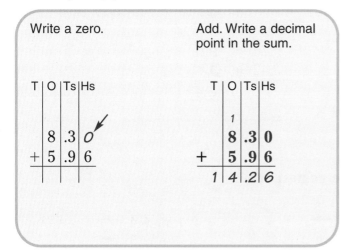

Write a zero.		Add. Write a decimal point in the sum.

T	O	Ts	Hs
	8	.3	0
+	5	.9	6

T	O	Ts	Hs
		1	
	8	.3	0
+	5	.9	6
1	4	.2	6

Find: 39.2 − 26.71

Write a zero.		Regroup. Subtract. Write a decimal point in the difference.

T	O	Ts	Hs
3	9	.2	0
− 2	6	.7	1

T	O	Ts	Hs
		11	
	8	1	10
3	9	.2	0
− 2	6	.7	1
1	2	.4	9

Add or subtract. Write zeros as needed.

a **b** **c** **d**

1.

T	O	Ts
1	1	
1	6	.2
+2	4	.9
4	1	.1

T	O	Ts
5	0	.6
+3	8	.4

T	O	Ts
	12	
6	2	11
7	3	.1
−2	5	.3
4	7	.8

T	O	Ts	Hs
$4	8	.5	0
− 3	0	.6	3

2.

```
  2.3 5 6
+8.6 7 9
```

```
  4.6 2 9
+3.4 7 5
```

```
2 4.6 1
−   2.8
```

```
8 7.5 9
−4 9
```

3.

```
$ 4 5.8 5
+   3 2.1 4
```

```
$ 2 6.1 8
+   1 3.7 5
```

```
3.7 5 7
−0.5 0 9
```

```
6 1.0 0 5
−5 7.3 7 6
```

4.

```
2 8.2 4
1 6.4 5
+1 4.2 3
```

```
7 8.0 9
2 5.1 0
+2 1 8.4 5
```

```
8
−0.5 2 9
```

```
9 6
−  4.0 0 1
```

Estimation of Decimal Sums and Differences

To estimate a decimal sum or difference, first round the decimals to the same place value. Then add or subtract the rounded numbers.

Estimate: 7.13 + 2.89

Round each decimal to the nearest one.
Add.

$$
\begin{array}{r}
7.13 \rightarrow \quad 7 \\
+2.89 \rightarrow +\ 3 \\
\hline
10
\end{array}
$$

Estimate: 9.26 − 3.42

Round each decimal to the nearest tenth.
Subtract.

$$
\begin{array}{r}
9.76 \rightarrow \quad 9.8 \\
-3.42 \rightarrow -3.4 \\
\hline
6.4
\end{array}
$$

Estimate each sum or difference by rounding to the nearest one.

	a	b	c
1.	$\begin{array}{r} 7.3 \rightarrow \quad 7 \\ +0.6 \rightarrow +\ 1 \\ \hline 8 \end{array}$	$\begin{array}{r} \$\ 2.5\ 6 \rightarrow \\ +\ 3.8\ 9 \rightarrow \\ \hline \end{array}$	$\begin{array}{r} \$\ 1\ 3.8\ 4 \rightarrow \\ +\qquad 7.6\ 3 \rightarrow \\ \hline \end{array}$
2.	$\begin{array}{r} 5.4 \rightarrow \\ -4.6 \rightarrow \\ \hline \end{array}$	$\begin{array}{r} \$\ 6.1\ 8 \rightarrow \\ -\ \ 2.5\ 9 \rightarrow \\ \hline \end{array}$	$\begin{array}{r} \$\ 8\ 2.6\ 4 \rightarrow \\ -\ \ 3\ 3.2\ 1 \rightarrow \\ \hline \end{array}$
3.	$\begin{array}{r} 2.9\ 4 \rightarrow \\ +3.8 \quad \rightarrow \\ \hline \end{array}$	$\begin{array}{r} 7.6 \quad \rightarrow \\ +5.2\ 7 \rightarrow \\ \hline \end{array}$	$\begin{array}{r} 5\ 3.8\ 7 \rightarrow \\ +1\ 2.9 \quad \rightarrow \\ \hline \end{array}$

Estimate each sum or difference by rounding to the nearest tenth.

	a	b	c
4.	$\begin{array}{r} 3.6\ 4 \rightarrow \quad 3.6 \\ +2.7\ 8 \rightarrow +2.8 \\ \hline \end{array}$	$\begin{array}{r} 5.4\ 5 \rightarrow \\ +1.7\ 4 \rightarrow \\ \hline \end{array}$	$\begin{array}{r} 2\ 7.2\ 6 \rightarrow \\ +1\ 4.3\ 5 \rightarrow \\ \hline \end{array}$
5.	$\begin{array}{r} 5\ 3.8\ 7 \rightarrow \\ +\quad 6\ 2.6 \quad \rightarrow \\ \hline \end{array}$	$\begin{array}{r} 4\ 8.6 \quad \rightarrow \\ -1\ 2.2\ 3 \rightarrow \\ \hline \end{array}$	$\begin{array}{r} 2.6 \quad \rightarrow \\ -0.5\ 9\ 4 \rightarrow \\ \hline \end{array}$

Problem-Solving Method: Work Backwards

Jerome has $646.15 in his bank account. During the last two weeks, he withdrew $115.28, deposited $83.30, and withdrew $62.97. How much did Jerome have in his account two weeks ago?

Understand the problem.

- **What do you want to know?**
  How much money was in Jerome's account two weeks ago?

- **What information is given?**
  There is $646.15 in the account now.
  He withdrew $115.28, deposited $83.30, and withdrew $62.97.

Plan how to solve it.

- **What method can you use?**
  You can work backwards. Work from the money in the account now to find the money in the account two weeks ago.

Solve it.

- **How can you use this method to solve the problem?**
  Addition and subtraction are opposite operations. So, add the amounts withdrawn and subtract the amount deposited.

$$
\begin{array}{ll}
\$646.15 \rightarrow & \text{amount in bank now} \\
+\ 115.28 \rightarrow & \text{amount withdrawn} \\
\hline
\$761.43 & \\
-\ \ \ 83.30 \rightarrow & \text{amount deposited} \\
\hline
\$678.13 & \\
+\ \ \ 62.97 \rightarrow & \text{amount withdrawn} \\
\hline
\$741.10 &
\end{array}
$$

- **What is the answer?**
  Two weeks ago, Jerome had $741.10 in his account.

Look back and check your answer.

- **Is your answer reasonable?**
  You can check by working forwards from the amount of money in the account two weeks ago.

$$
\begin{array}{l}
\$741.10 \\
-\ 115.28 \\
\hline
\$625.82 \\
+\ \ \ 83.30 \\
\hline
\$709.12 \\
-\ \ \ 62.97 \\
\hline
\$646.15
\end{array}
$$

The amount in his account and the answer match.
The answer is reasonable.

Work backwards to solve each problem.

1. Anne has $85.97 left over from her paycheck. She spent $117.43 for insurance and $49.05 for her phone bill. Then she spent $37.28 for groceries. How much was Anne's paycheck?

Answer_____

2. Sue is guessing her grandfather's age. He tells her that when you divide his age by 3 and then subtract 7, the result is 13. How old is Sue's grandfather?

Answer_____

3. Half of the students in Linda's class are girls. Half of the girls have blue eyes. Seven girls have blue eyes. How many students are in Linda's class?

Answer_____

4. Gabrielle used 18.5 centimeters of wire to make a bracelet. Then she made 2 earrings using 4.75 centimeters of wire for each one. She had 26.38 centimeters of wire left over. How much wire did Gabrielle start with?

Answer_____

5. The park cleanup started at 9:00 AM By noon, there were three times more people than had started. At 12:30, another 12 people arrived. Now there are 42 people in all. How many people started at 9:00 AM?

Answer_____

76

Write as a decimal.

                     a   *b*

1. sixty-seven thousandths _____   seventy-six hundredths _____

Write each decimal in words.

2. 42.615 _____

3. 0.078 _____

Write each money amount with a dollar sign and a decimal point.

4. sixty-eight dollars and twenty-seven cents _____

5. four hundred five dollars and three cents _____

Compare. Write <, >, or =. Write in zeros as needed.

       a   *b*   *c*

6. 0.52 _____ 0.25   0.213 _____ 0.123   1.806 _____ 1.860

Write in order from least to greatest.

                a   *b*

7. 0.5   0.052   0.25 _____   0.19   0.91   0.019 _____

Write each decimal as a fraction.

      a   *b*   *c*   *d*

8. 0.3 _____   0.25 _____   0.07 _____   0.8 _____

Write each decimal as a mixed number.

      a   *b*   *c*   *d*

9. 1.75 _____   5.2 _____   24.06 _____   16.75 _____

Write each fraction as a decimal.

      a   *b*   *c*   *d*

10. $\frac{108}{100}$ _____ $\frac{7}{10}$ _____ $\frac{3}{5}$ _____ $\frac{11}{25}$ _____

Write each mixed number as a decimal.

      a   *b*   *c*   *d*

11. $2\frac{7}{10}$ _____ $5\frac{3}{5}$ _____ $10\frac{1}{4}$ _____ $8\frac{3}{4}$ _____

Round to the nearest one.

	a	b	c	d
12.	7.6 _____	2.2 _____	3.8 _____	0.5 _____

Round each amount to the nearest dollar.

	a	b	c	d
13.	$7.95 _____	$4.27 _____	$9.03 _____	$15.49 _____

Round to the nearest tenth.

	a	b	c	d
14.	0.38 _____	0.19 _____	5.12 _____	72.09 _____

Add or subtract. Write zeros as needed.

a | b | c | d

15.

$$\begin{array}{r} 4\,2.7 \\ +6\,8.9 \\ \hline \end{array} \qquad \begin{array}{r} 3.0\,0\,1 \\ +0.9\,5\,7 \\ \hline \end{array} \qquad \begin{array}{r} \$\,2\,9.9\,5 \\ +\ \ 5\,6.4\,9 \\ \hline \end{array} \qquad \begin{array}{r} 6\,8.5 \\ +\ \ 0.8\,1\,4 \\ \hline \end{array}$$

16.

$$\begin{array}{r} \$\,1\,6.1\,5 \\ 3\,9.0\,6 \\ +\ \ 3\,4.7\,9 \\ \hline \end{array} \qquad \begin{array}{r} 1 \\ -0.8\,1 \\ \hline \end{array} \qquad \begin{array}{r} 4\,0 \\ -\ \ 0.3\,6\,1 \\ \hline \end{array} \qquad \begin{array}{r} 1\,1\,3.5 \\ 3\,6.9 \\ +2\,0\,7.4\,6 \\ \hline \end{array}$$

Estimate each sum or difference by rounding to the nearest one.

a | b | c | d

17.

$$\begin{array}{r} 4.1 \rightarrow \\ +9.8 \rightarrow \\ \hline \end{array} \qquad \begin{array}{r} 6.5 \rightarrow \\ +3.7 \rightarrow \\ \hline \end{array} \qquad \begin{array}{r} 9\,4.7 \rightarrow \\ -1\,6.4 \rightarrow \\ \hline \end{array} \qquad \begin{array}{r} 1\,1.3\,2 \rightarrow \\ -\ \ 8.2\ \ \rightarrow \\ \hline \end{array}$$

Estimate each sum or difference by rounding to the nearest tenth.

a | b | c | d

18.

$$\begin{array}{r} 1.3\,6 \rightarrow \\ +8.2\,5 \rightarrow \\ \hline \end{array} \qquad \begin{array}{r} 5.6\,4 \rightarrow \\ +7.0\,2 \rightarrow \\ \hline \end{array} \qquad \begin{array}{r} 6.7\,9 \rightarrow \\ -4.1\,4 \rightarrow \\ \hline \end{array} \qquad \begin{array}{r} 2\,5.6\,8 \rightarrow \\ -1\,2.4\,9 \rightarrow \\ \hline \end{array}$$

Use logic to solve each problem.

19. Donovan Bailey, Leroy Burrell, and Carl Lewis are among the fastest-running men on Earth. Their times for the 100-meter dash are 9.86 seconds, $10\frac{17}{20}$ seconds, and 9.84 seconds. Burrell's time has a 5 in the hundredths place. Bailey is faster than Lewis. Whose time is the fastest?

DB

10.85

Bailey
9.84

9.86

Answer _Bailey_

20. The three tallest trees in the United States measure 100.3 meters, 95.4 meters, and $83\frac{22}{25}$ meters. One of the trees is a Douglas fir. The other two trees are a redwood and a giant sequoia. The sequoia has a 4 in the tenths place. The redwood is not the tallest. What are the heights of the three trees?

100.3
Douglas   95.4 | 83.88
sequoia
redwood

Douglas fir _100.3 m_
Redwood _83.88_
Giant sequoia _95.4_

Work backwards to solve each problem.

21. Celia's model train set now has 68.3 feet of tracks. After she bought it, she added 24.65 feet of tracks. But it was too long for the room. She then took off 9.7 feet. How many feet of tracks came with Celia's train set when she bought it?

+68.3
9.7
78.0

78
24.65
54.65

Answer _54.65_

22. Sean spent a total of $106.43 for the team party. He paid $6.98 for invitations and $74.25 for food and drinks. He spent the rest of the money on decorations. How much did Sean pay for the decorations?

6.98
+74.25
92.13

106.43
-92.13
14.30

Answer _$14.30_

unit 5
multiplication and Division of Decimals

Multiplying by Powers of 10

To multiply decimals by **powers of ten**, move the decimal point in the product to the right as many places as there are zeros in the multiplier.

Remember, sometimes you might need to write zeros in the product in order to move the decimal point the correct number of places.

Study these examples.

$10 \times 0.24 = 2.4$ $100 \times 0.54 = 54$ $1,000 \times 0.36 = 360$

$10 \times 0.245 = 2.45$ $100 \times 0.545 = 54.5$ $1,000 \times 0.367 = 367$

$10 \times 2.4 = 24$ $100 \times 5.4 = 540$ $1,000 \times 3.670 = 3,670$

$10 \times 2.04 = 20.4$ $100 \times 5.04 = 504$ $1,000 \times 3.067 = 3,067$

Multiply. Write zeros as needed.

a

1. $0.58 \times 10 = \underline{\quad 5.8 \quad}$ $5.8 \times 10 = \underline{58.0}$ $0.058 \times 10 = \underline{0.58}$

2. $7.5 \times 10 = \underline{75.0}$ $0.83 \times 10 = \underline{8.3}$ $4.6 \times 10 = \underline{46.0}$

3. $2.8 \times 100 = \underline{280.0}$ $0.7 \times 100 = \underline{7.0}$ $0.07 \times 100 = \underline{7.0}$

4. $4.6 \times 1,000 = \underline{4600.0}$ $6.2 \times 1,000 = \underline{62000}$ $0.075 \times 1,000 = \underline{75.0}$

5. $3.1 \times 10 = \underline{31.0}$ $3.1 \times 100 = \underline{310.0}$ $3.15 \times 1,000 = \underline{3150.0}$

Multiplying Decimals by Whole Numbers

To multiply decimals by whole numbers, multiply the same way as whole numbers.
Place the decimal point in the product by counting the numbers of decimal places in each factor.
The product will have the same number of decimal places.

Find: 18 × 2.3

Multiply. Write the decimal point in the product.

```
    2.3        1 decimal place
 ×   18       +0 decimal places
   184
    23
   41.4        1 decimal place
```

Find: 63 × 0.128

Multiply. Write the decimal point in the product.

```
   0.128       3 decimal places
 ×    63      +0 decimal places
   384
   768
   8.064        3 decimal places
```

Multiply. Write zeros as needed.

	a	b	c	d
1.	0.2 × 8 1.6	0.2 4 × 4 0.98	4.7 × 5 23.5	3.0 9 2 × 6 18.552
2.	3 2 ×0.0 4 1.28	4 0 7 × 2.8 3250 + 8140 11 3 9.0	0.2 3 1 × 4 7 1 6 1 7 + 9 2 4 0 10.8 5 7	4 3 7 ×0.0 0 2 8.74
3.	3.0 0 2 × 2 6	0.2 0 5 × 3 5	3 6 8 ×0.0 3 2	1.1 0 1 × 8 0 9

Line up the digits. Then find the products. Write zeros as needed.

a
4. 41 × 15.4 = _____

```
  1 5.4
× 4 1
```

b
16 × 4.3 = _____

c
112 × 448.5 = _____

Multiplying Decimals by Decimals

To multiply decimals by decimals, multiply the same way as whole numbers. Place the decimal point in the product by counting the number of decimal places in each factor. The product will have the same number of decimal places.

Remember, sometimes you might need to write a zero in the product in order to place the decimal point correctly.

Find: 0.92×15.4

Multiply. Write the decimal point in the product.

$$
\begin{array}{r}
0.92 \\
\times 15.4 \\
\hline
368 \\
460 \\
092 \\
\hline
14.168
\end{array}
\qquad
\begin{array}{l}
\text{2 places} \\
\text{+1 place} \\
\hline
\\
\\
\text{3 places}
\end{array}
$$

Find: 0.49×0.05

Multiply. Write the decimal point in the product.

$$
\begin{array}{r}
0.49 \\
\times\ 0.05 \\
\hline
245 \\
000 \\
\hline
0.0245
\end{array}
\qquad
\begin{array}{l}
\text{2 places} \\
\text{+2 places} \\
\hline
\\
\text{4 places}
\end{array}
$$

Write a zero.

Multiply. Write zeros as needed.

	a	b	c	d
1.	$\begin{array}{r}0.5\\\times0.8\\\hline 0.40\end{array}$	$\begin{array}{r}0.6\\\times0.9\\\hline\end{array}$	$\begin{array}{r}5.2\\\times0.7\\\hline\end{array}$	$\begin{array}{r}9.6\\\times0.4\\\hline\end{array}$
2.	$\begin{array}{r}0.62\\\times\ 0.5\\\hline\end{array}$	$\begin{array}{r}0.12\\\times\ 0.3\\\hline\end{array}$	$\begin{array}{r}0.05\\\times\ 0.6\\\hline\end{array}$	$\begin{array}{r}0.16\\\times\ 0.2\\\hline\end{array}$
3.	$\begin{array}{r}0.48\\\times6.95\\\hline\end{array}$	$\begin{array}{r}0.76\\\times43.5\\\hline\end{array}$	$\begin{array}{r}0.56\\\times9.12\\\hline\end{array}$	$\begin{array}{r}0.24\\\times18.7\\\hline\end{array}$

Line up the digits. Then find the products. Write zeros as needed.

	a	b	c
4.	$0.137 \times 0.06 =$ _____	$1.284 \times 0.48 =$ _____	$4.507 \times 0.52 =$ _____

$$
\begin{array}{r}
0.137 \\
\times 0.06 \\
\hline
\end{array}
$$

Problem-Solving Method: Identify Extra Information

The planet Mercury is 36,000,000 miles from the sun. It orbits, or circles, the sun faster than any other planet. At a speed of 29.76 miles per second, it only takes Mercury 87.969 days to orbit the sun. How far does Mercury travel in 1 minute?

Understand the problem.

- **What do you want to know?**
  how far Mercury travels in 1 minute (60 seconds)

- **What information is given?**
  Mercury's distance from the sun, the miles per second, and the days to complete a full orbit

Plan how to solve it.

- **What method can you use?**
  You can identify extra information that is not needed to solve the problem.

Solve it.

- **How can you use this method to solve the problem?**
  Reread the problem. Cross out any unnecessary facts. Then you can focus on the needed facts to solve the problem.

  > ~~The planet Mercury is 36,000,000 miles from the sun. It orbits, or circles, the sun faster than any other planet.~~ At a speed of 29.76 miles per second, ~~it only takes Mercury 87.969 days to orbit the sun.~~ How far does Mercury travel in 1 minute?

- **What is the answer?**

  29.76 × 60 = 1,785.6

  In 1 minute, Mercury travels 1,785.6 miles.

Look back and check your answer.

- **Is your answer reasonable?**
  You can estimate to check your answer.

  30 × 60 = 1,800

  The estimate is close to the answer.
  The answer is reasonable.

In each problem, cross out the extra information. Then solve the problem.

1. Earth is 92.96 million miles from the sun. It orbits the sun in about 365.26 days, traveling at an average speed of 18.51 miles per second. How far does Earth travel in 1 minute? (60 seconds)

Answer _____

2. Fleas can jump up to 150 times the length of their bodies. This is equivalent to a person jumping nearly 1,000 feet. The average flea is about 0.2 inch long. How high can it jump?

Answer _____

3. Fingernails grow about 0.004 inch a day. After not cutting his nails for 44 years, a man in India has the world's longest nails. His thumbnail is 4.67 feet long. How many inches do fingernails grow in 1 week? (7 days)

Answer _____

4. Every day, 274,000 carats of diamonds are mined. One carat is 0.02 grams. The Cullinan Diamond is the largest diamond ever discovered. It is 3,106 carats. How many grams does the Cullinan Diamond weigh?

Answer _____

5. The movie *Forrest Gump* earned a total of $679.7 million worldwide. $329.7 million of that total was made in the United States. *Forrest Gump* was nominated for 13 Academy Awards and won 6. How much of its total earnings were made outside the U.S.?

Answer _____

6. At 179.6 feet, the "Rattler" is one of the world's tallest wooden roller coasters. Each ride is 2.25 minutes long. "Superman the Escape" is one of the world's tallest steel roller coasters, at 415 feet. Its ride lasts 0.467 minutes. How much longer is a ride on the "Rattler" than on "Superman"?

Answer _____

Dividing by Powers of 10

To divide a decimal by a power of ten, move the decimal point in the dividend to the left as many places as there are zeros in the divisor.

Remember, sometimes you might need to write zeros in the quotient in order to correctly insert the decimal point.

Study these examples.

$0.75 \div 10 = 0.075$ $0.35 \div 100 = 0.0035$ $0.91 \div 1,000 = 0.00091$

$0.715 \div 10 = 0.0715$ $0.315 \div 100 = 0.00315$ $0.315 \div 1,000 = 0.000315$

$7.5 \div 10 = 0.75$ $3.5 \div 100 = 0.035$ $3.5 \div 1,000 = 0.0035$

$7.05 \div 10 = 0.705$ $3.05 \div 100 = 0.0305$ $3.05 \div 1,000 = 0.00305$

Divide. Write zeros as needed.

	a	b	c
1.	$6.89 \div 10 =$ _0.689_	$0.7 \div 10 =$ _____	$0.56 \div 10 =$ _____
2.	$12.3 \div 10 =$ _____	$0.49 \div 10 =$ _____	$8.1 \div 10 =$ _____
3.	$14.11 \div 100 =$ _____	$0.03 \div 100 =$ _____	$2.89 \div 100 =$ _____
4.	$37.737 \div 1,000 =$ _____	$9.91 \div 1,000 =$ _____	$134.2 \div 1,000 =$ _____
5.	$0.039 \div 10 =$ _____	$555.5 \div 100 =$ _____	$7.15 \div 1,000 =$ _____

Dividing Decimals by Whole Numbers

To divide a decimal by a whole number, write the decimal
point in the quotient directly above the decimal in the dividend.
Then divide the same way as you divide whole numbers.

Find: $11.88 ÷ 12

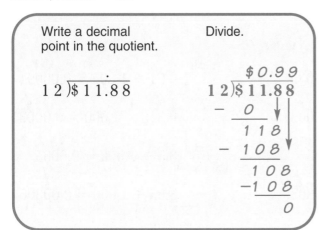

Write a decimal
point in the quotient.

$$12\overline{)\$11.88}$$

Divide.

$$
\begin{array}{r}
\$0.99 \\
12\overline{)\$11.88} \\
-0\downarrow \\
\hline
118 \\
-108\downarrow \\
\hline
108 \\
-108 \\
\hline
0
\end{array}
$$

Divide.

	a	b	c	d

1.

$$
\begin{array}{r}
2.2 \\
3\overline{)6.6} \\
-6\downarrow \\
\hline
0\,6 \\
-0\,6 \\
\hline
0
\end{array}
$$

b. $4\overline{)18.4}$

c. $9\overline{)\$5.76}$

d. $8\overline{)12.8}$

2.

$22\overline{)26.4}$

$19\overline{)96.9}$

$45\overline{)234.0}$

$25\overline{)\$6.50}$

Set up the problems. Then find the quotients.

a	b	c

3. 37.68 ÷ 60 = _____   543.20 ÷ 10 = _____   31.35 ÷ 57 = _____

$60\overline{)37.68}$

Dividing Decimals by Decimals

To divide a decimal by a decimal, change the divisor to a whole number by moving the decimal point. Move the decimal point in the dividend the same number of places. Then divide.

Remember, write a decimal point in the quotient directly above the position of the *new* decimal point in the dividend.

Find: 8.64 ÷ 0.6

Move each decimal point 1 place.

Divide.

$$0.6\overline{)8.6\,4}$$

```
      1 4.4
  6)8 6.4
   -6
    2 6
   -2 4
      2 4
     -2 4
        0
```

Find: 0.5280 ÷ 0.96

Move each decimal point 2 places.

Divide.

$$0.96\overline{)0.5\,2\,8\,0}$$

```
        0.5 5
  9 6)5 2.8 0
     -4 8 0
        4 8 0
       -4 8 0
            0
```

Divide.

a b c d

1.
```
        2.6
  3.4)8.8 4
    -6 8
     2 0 4
    -2 0 4
          0
```

$$0.9\overline{)1\,5.3}$$

$$0.7\overline{)4.0\,6}$$

$$1.5\overline{)4.9\,5}$$

2.
$$6.1\overline{)3\,2.9\,4}$$

$$3.9\overline{)2\,9.6\,4}$$

$$8.4\overline{)1\,0\,5.8\,4}$$

$$7.3\overline{)5\,7\,0.1\,3}$$

Set up the problems. Then find the quotients.

a b c

3. 6.12 ÷ 3.4 = _____

1.328 ÷ 0.8 = _____

333.32 ÷ 5.2 = _____

Dividing Whole Numbers by Decimals

To divide a whole number by a decimal, change the divisor to a whole number by moving the decimal point. To move the decimal point in the dividend the same number of places, you will need to add one or more zeros. Then divide.

Find: 48 ÷ 3.2

Move each decimal point 1 place.

$$3.2\overline{)4\,8.0}$$

Divide.

```
      1 5
32)4 8 0
  -3 2
   1 6 0
  -1 6 0
       0
```

Find: 39 ÷ 0.13

Move each decimal point 2 places.

$$0.13\overline{)3\,9.00}$$

Divide.

```
       3 0 0
13)3,9 0 0
  -3 9
     0 0
   -  0
       0 0
     -  0
         0
```

Divide. Write zeros as needed.

	a	b	c	d

1.

a.
```
      4
0.5)2.0
  -2 0
     0
```

b. $0.6\overline{)5\,4}$

c. $1.3\overline{)7\,8}$

d. $4.5\overline{)6\,7\,5}$

2.

a. $0.1\,4\overline{)8\,4}$

b. $0.3\,6\overline{)9\,7\,2}$

c. $0.9\,9\overline{)3,4\,6\,5}$

d. $7.2\overline{)1\,3,1\,7\,6}$

Set up the problems. Then find the quotients.

	a	b	c

3. 288 ÷ 0.8 = _____   636 ÷ 1.2 = _____   4,698 ÷ 0.54 = _____

Decimal Quotients

Often when you divide, your answer will have a remainder.
You can add zeros in the dividend and continue to divide until the
remainder is zero. If the dividend is a whole number, add a decimal
point and add zeros as needed.

Remember, zeros also may be needed in the quotient.

Find: 26.7 ÷ 4

Divide until you have a remainder.

```
      6.6
 4)2 6.7
  -2 4↓
     2 7
    -2 4
       3
```

Add zeros.

```
      6.6 7 5
 4)2 6.7 0 0
  -2 4↓
     2 7
    -2 4↓
       3 0
      -2 8↓
         2 0
        -2 0
           0
```

Find: 802 ÷ 4

Divide until you have a remainder

```
      2 0 0
 4)8 0 2
  -8↓
    0 0
   - 0↓
     0 2
```

Add a decimal point and a zero.

```
      2 0 0.5
 4)8 0 2.0
  -8↓
    0 0↓
   - 0↓
     0 2
    - 0↓
       2 0
      -2 0
         0
```

Divide. Write zeros as needed.

a   b   c   d

1.

a)
```
      2.0 7 5
 4)8.3 0 0
  -8↓
    0 3
   - 0↓
     3 0
    -2 8↓
       2 0
      -2 0
         0
```

b) 5)5 7.1

c) 9)1 8.6 3

d) 6)0.6 5 7 0

2.

a)
```
        1.7 5
 3 2)5 6.0 0
    -3 2↓
     2 4 0↓
    -2 2 4↓
       1 6 0
      -1 6 0
           0
```

b) 4 0)8 5 0

c) 1 8)4 5

d) 8 5)8,7 0 4

Rounding Quotients

Sometimes when you have a remainder, adding zeros to the dividend and continuing to divide will result in a remainder of zero. Sometimes the remainder will never be zero, or may take too many steps. You may need to round the quotient. You may also need to round the quotient when you are dividing money.

Find: 23 ÷ 7.1

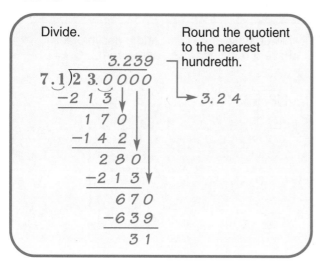

Find: $1.85 ÷ 10

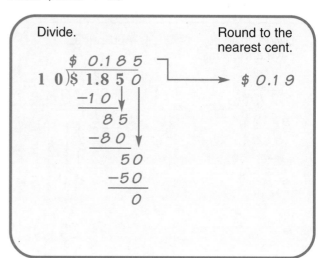

Divide. Round to the place named.

	a	*b*	*c*
	nearest tenth	nearest hundredth	nearest tenth

1.

```
        6.27→6.3
5.1)3 2.0 0 0
   −3 0 6
     1 4 0
    −1 0 2
       3 8 0
      −3 5 7
         2 3
```

```
3)2 2
```

```
8)6.4 8
```

	nearest cent	nearest cent	nearest dollar

2.

```
   $ 0.3 2 5→$ 0.3 3
6)$ 1.9 5 0
 −1 8
   1 5
  −1 2
     3 0
```

```
1 0)$ 4 0 5.7 5
```

```
2 9)$ 6 0 8
```

Problem-Solving Method: Complete a Pattern

Earth's oldest living organisms are bristlecone pine trees. One found in California is almost 5,000 years old. Bristlecones are also one of Earth's slowest growers, at only 0.0003 inch a day. How many days does it take the tree to grow 12 inches (1 foot)?

Understand the problem.

- **What do you want to know?**
  how many days it takes a bristlecone to grow 12 inches

- **What information is given?**
  They grow 0.0003 inch a day.

Plan how to solve it.

- **What method can you use?**
  You can find and complete a pattern.

Solve it.

- **How can you use this method to solve the problem?**
  Start with a basic division fact. Then follow the pattern in the decimal points to find 12 ÷ 0.0003.

12	÷	3	=	4	← Basic Fact
12	÷	0.3	=	40	
12	÷	0.03	=	400	
12	÷	0.003	=	4,000	
12	÷	0.0003	=	40,000	

Decimal point moves 4 places to the **left**. Decimal point moves 4 places to the **right**.

- **What is the answer?**
  It takes 40,000 days for a bristlecone pine tree to grow 12 inches.

Look back and check your answer.

- **Is your answer reasonable?**
  You can check your division with multiplication.

$$
\begin{array}{r}
40,000 \\
\times\ 0.0003 \\
\hline
12.0000
\end{array}
$$

The product matches the dividend.
The answer is reasonable.

Complete a pattern to solve each problem.

1. Human hair grows about 0.02 inch a day. How many days does it take hair to grow 6 inches?

$$6 \div 2 = \underline{\quad 3 \quad}$$
$$6 \div 0.2 = \underline{\quad 30 \quad}$$
$$6 \div 0.02 = \underline{\qquad\qquad}$$

Answer _____

2. A garden snail moves only 0.03 miles per hour. How far can a snail move in 8 hours?

$$8 \times 3 = \underline{\qquad\qquad}$$
$$8 \times 0.3 = \underline{\qquad\qquad}$$
$$8 \times 0.03 = \underline{\qquad\qquad}$$

Answer _____

3. One milliliter is equal to 0.001 of a liter. How many milliliters are in a 2-liter bottle of soda?

$$2 \div 1 = \underline{\qquad\qquad}$$
$$2 \div 0.1 = \underline{\qquad\qquad}$$
$$2 \div 0.01 = \underline{\qquad\qquad}$$
$$2 \div 0.001 = \underline{\qquad\qquad}$$

Answer _____

4. In a certain week, one Japanese yen was worth 0.008 United States dollars. How many United States dollars could you get for 10 yen?

$$10 \times 8 = \underline{\qquad\qquad}$$
$$10 \times 0.8 = \underline{\qquad\qquad}$$
$$10 \times 0.08 = \underline{\qquad\qquad}$$
$$10 \times 0.008 = \underline{\qquad\qquad}$$

Answer _____

5. One nickel is worth 0.05 of a dollar. How many nickels do you need to have $15.00?

$$15 \div 5 = \underline{\qquad\qquad}$$
$$15 \div 0.5 = \underline{\qquad\qquad}$$
$$15 \div 0.05 = \underline{\qquad\qquad}$$

Answer _____

6. In some places, sales tax is 0.05 times the price of an item. If a hat costs $9.00, how much sales tax will be charged?

$$9 \times 5 = \underline{\qquad\qquad}$$
$$9 \times 0.5 = \underline{\qquad\qquad}$$
$$9 \times 0.05 = \underline{\qquad\qquad}$$

Answer _____

Multiply. Write zeros as needed.

	a	b	c

1. $2.31 \times 10 =$ _____ $0.56 \times 100 =$ _____ $7.8 \times 1,000 =$ _____

2. $0.83 \times 10 =$ _____ $6.4 \times 100 =$ _____ $0.38 \times 1,000 =$ _____

Multiply. Write zeros as needed.

	a	b	c	d

3.
$$\begin{array}{r} 7.2\,3 \\ \times\quad 2 \\ \hline \end{array} \qquad \begin{array}{r} 6 \\ \times 5.0\,1\,4 \\ \hline \end{array} \qquad \begin{array}{r} \$\,0.6\,7 \\ \times\qquad 3 \\ \hline \end{array} \qquad \begin{array}{r} 8 \\ \times 0.9\,1 \\ \hline \end{array}$$

4.
$$\begin{array}{r} 6\,8 \\ \times\ 0.0\,5 \\ \hline \end{array} \qquad \begin{array}{r} 5\,7\,4 \\ \times\quad 3.7 \\ \hline \end{array} \qquad \begin{array}{r} 0.9\,3\,1 \\ \times\qquad 7\,5 \\ \hline \end{array} \qquad \begin{array}{r} \$\,1\,6.9\,9 \\ \times\qquad 1\,2 \\ \hline \end{array}$$

5.
$$\begin{array}{r} 0.9 \\ \times 0.5 \\ \hline \end{array} \qquad \begin{array}{r} 3.6 \\ \times 0.7 \\ \hline \end{array} \qquad \begin{array}{r} 1.6 \\ \times 8.4 \\ \hline \end{array} \qquad \begin{array}{r} 1\,2.7 \\ \times\ \ 6.3 \\ \hline \end{array}$$

6.
$$\begin{array}{r} 4.2\,7 \\ \times 0.0\,2 \\ \hline \end{array} \qquad \begin{array}{r} 0.0\,5\,5 \\ \times\ \ 1.0\,8 \\ \hline \end{array} \qquad \begin{array}{r} 6.7 \\ \times 9.3 \\ \hline \end{array} \qquad \begin{array}{r} 0.9\,3\,1 \\ \times\qquad 5.8 \\ \hline \end{array}$$

Line up the digits. Then find the products. Write zeros as needed.

	a	b	c

7. $17 \times 2.5 =$ _____ $25 \times 7.3 =$ _____ $32 \times 41.5 =$ _____

8. $0.63 \times 0.5 =$ _____ $0.29 \times 1.84 =$ _____ $3.18 \times 1.54 =$ _____

Divide. Write zeros as needed.

	a	b	c
9.	$0.34 \div 10 =$ _____	$0.92 \div 100 =$ _____	$1.58 \div 1,000 =$ _____
10.	$0.05 \div 10 =$ _____	$1.9 \div 100 =$ _____	$6.495 \div 1,000 =$ _____

Divide.

a　　　　　　　　　b　　　　　　　　　c　　　　　　　　　d

11.

$7\overline{)9.1}$ 　　　　 $5\overline{)3\ 1.5}$ 　　　　 $4\overline{)\$\ 3\ 0.4\ 0}$ 　　　　 $8\overline{)1\ 6.8}$

12.

$2.6\overline{)3.9}$ 　　　　 $0.9\overline{)1\ 9.8}$ 　　　　 $0.1\ 6\overline{)3.0\ 4}$ 　　　　 $8.2\overline{)2\ 1\ 7.3}$

13.

$5.6\overline{)1,6\ 8\ 0}$ 　　　　 $0.8\overline{)1\ 6}$ 　　　　 $2.5\overline{)2,8\ 2\ 0}$ 　　　　 $3.4\overline{)1,5\ 9\ 8}$

Divide. Round to the value named.

a　　　　　　　　　　b　　　　　　　　　　c

nearest tenth　　　　　　nearest cent　　　　　nearest hundredth

14.

$2.3\overline{)2.8\ 7\ 5}$ 　　　　 $7\overline{)\$\ 1\ 5.0\ 2}$ 　　　　 $5\overline{)1.7\ 3\ 2}$

UNIT 5 Review

In each problem, cross out the extra information. Then solve the problem.

15. Pluto is the farthest planet from the sun, at 5.9 billion kilometers. It takes Pluto 90.950 days to orbit the sun at a speed of 4.74 kilometers per second. How far does Pluto travel in 30 seconds?

Answer_____

16. In 1996, 31.9% of students in the United States had access to a computer. The average student that year used a computer 5.3 hours a week. How many hours did the average student use a computer each day in 1996? Round the answer to the nearest tenth. (1 week = 7 days)

Answer_____

17. In-line skates were introduced to the United States in the late 1970s. In 1998, the record for the highest speed on in-line skates was set at 64.02 miles per hour. How far could a person skate in 2 hours at this speed?

Answer_____

18. On December 17, 1903, Orville Wright became the first man to fly an engine-powered airplane. His flight took place near Kitty Hawk, North Carolina, and covered 120 feet in 0.2 minutes. On average, how many feet per minute did the plane fly?

Answer_____

Find and complete a pattern to solve each problem.

19. One cup is about 0.06 of a gallon. How many cups of water do you need to fill a 54-gallon fish tank?

54	÷	6	=	_____
54	÷	0.6	=	_____
54	÷	0.06	=	_____

Answer_____

20. A lamp with one bulb costs an average of $0.02 per hour for electricity. If you leave a lamp turned on for 12 hours, how much will it cost?

12	×	2	=	_____
12	×	0.2	=	_____
12	×	0.02	=	_____

Answer_____

unit 6
measurement

Customary Length

The customary units that are used to measure length are **inch, foot, yard,** and **mile**. The chart gives the relationship of one unit to another.

You can multiply or divide to change units of measurement.

To compare two measurements, first change them to the same unit.

1 foot (ft.)	=	12 inches (in.)
1 yard (yd.)	=	3 ft.
	=	36 in.
1 mile (mi.)	=	1,760 yd.
	=	5,280 ft.

Find: $3\frac{1}{2}$ ft. = _____ in.

To change larger units to smaller units, multiply.

$$1 \text{ ft.} = 12 \text{ in.}$$
$$3\frac{1}{2} \times 12 = \frac{7}{2} \times 12 = 42$$
$$3\frac{1}{2} \text{ ft.} = 42 \text{ in.}$$

Find: 10 ft. = _____ yd.

To change smaller units to larger units, divide.

$$3 \text{ ft.} = 1 \text{ yd.}$$
$$10 \div 3 = 3\frac{1}{3}$$
$$10 \text{ ft.} = 3\frac{1}{3} \text{ yd.}$$

Change each measurement to the smaller unit.

a   b   c

1. $5\frac{1}{6}$ yd. = _____ ft. $1\frac{1}{2}$ mi. = _____ ft. $7\frac{1}{3}$ ft. = _____ in.

2. $1\frac{1}{4}$ yd. = _____ in.   21 yd. = _____ ft.   4 mi. = _____ yd.

Change each measurement to the larger unit.

a   b   c

3. 51 in. = _____ ft.   38 ft. = _____ yd.   .   60 in. = _____ ft.

4. 4,400 yd. = _____ mi.   222 in. = _____ ft.   15,840 ft. = _____ mi.

Compare. Write <, >, or =.

a   b

5. 24 in. _____<_____ 4 ft.   3 mi. _____ 10,000 ft.
   1 ft. = 12 in.
   4 ft. = 4 × 12 = 48 in.

6. 12 ft. _____ 4 yd.   3,600 yd. _____ 2 mi.

Customary Weight

The customary units that are used to measure weight are **ounce, pound,** and **ton**. The chart shows the relationship of one unit to another.

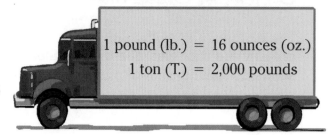

1 pound (lb.) = 16 ounces (oz.)
1 ton (T.) = 2,000 pounds

Find: $5\frac{1}{2}$ **lb.** = _____ **oz.**

To change larger units to smaller units, multiply.

1 lb. = 16 oz.

$5\frac{1}{2} \times 16 = \frac{11}{2} \times 16 = 88$

$5\frac{1}{2}$ lb. = 88 oz.

Find: 6,500 lb. = _____ **T.**

To change smaller units to larger units, divide.

2,000 lb. = 1 T.

$6,500 \div 2,000 = 3\frac{1}{4}$

$6,500$ lb = $3\frac{1}{4}$ T.

Change each measurement to the smaller unit.

a	b	c
1. $3\frac{1}{4}$ lb. = _____ oz.	$2\frac{1}{2}$ T. = _____ lb.	6 lb. = _____ oz.
2. 4 T. = _____ lb.	$1\frac{3}{8}$ lb. = _____ oz.	$4\frac{3}{16}$ lb. = _____ oz.

Change each measurement to the larger unit.

a	b	c
3. 53 oz. = _____ lb.	7,000 lb. = _____ T.	80 oz. = _____ lb.
4. 72 oz. = _____ lb.	36 oz. = _____ lb.	2,400 lb. = _____ T.

Compare. Write <, >, or =.

a

5. 40 lb. _____ 640 oz.

1 lb. = 16 oz.
40 lb. = 40 × 16 = 640 oz.

b

10,000 lb. _____ 4 T.

6. $6\frac{1}{2}$ lb. _____ 100 oz.

$\frac{1}{8}$ T. _____ 300 lb.

Customary Capacity

The customary units that are used to measure **capacity** are **cup, pint, quart,** and **gallon**. The chart shows the relationship of one unit to another.

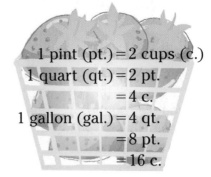

1 pint (pt.) = 2 cups (c.)
1 quart (qt.) = 2 pt.
= 4 c.
1 gallon (gal.) = 4 qt.
= 8 pt.
= 16 c.

Find: $3\frac{3}{4}$ **qt. =** _____ **c.**

To change larger units to smaller units, multiply.

1 qt. = 4 c.

$3\frac{3}{4} \times 4 = \frac{15}{4} \times 4 = 15$

$3\frac{3}{4}$ qt. = 15 c.

Find: **21 qt. =** _____ **gal.**

To change smaller units to larger units, divide.

4 qt. = 1 gal.

$21 \div 4 = 5\frac{1}{4}$

21 qt. = $5\frac{1}{4}$ gal.

Change each measurement to the smaller unit.

	a	b	c
1.	$8\frac{1}{2}$ pt. = _____ c.	$2\frac{1}{4}$ gal. = _____ qt.	13 qt. = _____ pt.
2.	$4\frac{1}{8}$ gal. = _____ pt.	9 qt. = _____ c.	$1\frac{1}{2}$ gal. = _____ c.

Change each measurement to the larger unit.

	a	b	c
3.	7 c. = _____ qt.	21 pt. = _____ gal.	11 c. = _____ pt.
4.	24 qt. = _____ gal.	14 pt. = _____ qt.	54 c. = _____ gal.

Compare. Write <, >, or =.

	a	b
5.	12 c. ___>___ 5 pt.	50 gal. _____ 2,000 qt.

1 pt. = 2 c
5 pt. = 5 × 2 = 10 c.

6.	$5\frac{1}{2}$ qt. _____ 22 c.	15.6 pt. _____ 2 gal.

Computing Measures

You can add, subtract, multiply, and divide measures that are given in two units. For example, 1 yd. 5 in. uses 2 units to measure one length.

Find: 1 lb. 14 oz. + 6 lb. 10 oz.

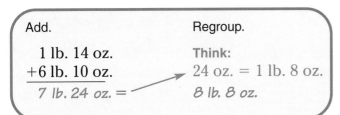

Find: 5 × 4 gal. 3 qt.

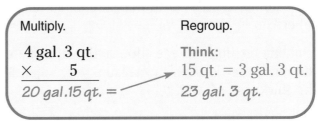

Find: 12 ft. 4 in. − 6 ft. 9 in.

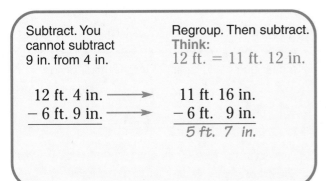

Find: 8 T. 200 lb. ÷ 6

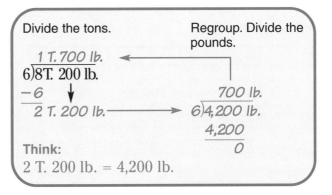

Find each answer.

	a	b	c
1.	5 gal. 2 qt. +2 gal. 3 qt. *7 gal. 5 qt. = 8 gal. 1 qt.*	9 ft. 6 in. +4 ft. 8 in.	7 yd. 1 ft. +3 yd. 2 ft.
2.	8 yd. 1 ft. −6 yd. 2 ft.	5 gal. 2 qt. −3 gal. 3 qt.	18 lb. 6 oz. × 4 oz.
3.	5 ft. 8 in. × 7 in.	8)10 lb. 8 oz.	7)9 yd. 1 ft.

Metric Length

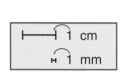

The **meter** (m) is the basic metric unit of length. A meter can be measured with a meter stick. The length of your arm is about 0.7 m.

A **centimeter** (cm) is one hundredth of a meter. (*Centi* means 0.01.) The centimeter is used to measure small lengths. The width of a paper clip is about 1 cm.

A **millimeter** (mm) is one thousandth of a meter. (*Milli* means 0.001.) The millimeter is used to measure very small lengths. The thickness of a nickel is about 2 mm.

A **kilometer** (km) is one thousand meters. (*Kilo* means 1,000.) The kilometer is used to measure long distances. The distance between two cities can be measured in kilometers.

⊢──⌢ 1 cm	
⌢ 1 mm	

1 km = 1,000 m
1 m = 100 cm
1 cm = 10 mm

1 m = 0.001 km
1 cm = 0.01 m
1 mm = 0.1 cm

Find: 8.2 m = _____ cm

To change larger units to smaller units, multiply.

$$1\ m = 100\ cm$$
$$8.2 \times 100 = 820$$
$$8.2\ m = 820\ cm$$

Find: 63 m = _____ km

To change smaller units to larger units, divide.

$$1,000\ m = 1\ km$$
$$63 \div 1,000 = 0.063$$
$$63\ m = 0.063\ km$$

Circle the best measurement.

a
1. length of a snail

    2 cm   2 m

2. width of a paper clip

    8 mm   8 cm

b
distance from Boston to New York

    300 m   300 km

length of a car

    5 cm   5 m

Change each measurement to the smaller unit.

a	b	c
3. 14.5 km = _____ m	7.25 m = _____ cm	18 cm = _____ mm
4. 3.4 m = _____ cm	21 m = _____ mm	0.9 km = _____ m

Change each measurement to the larger unit.

a	b	c
5. 48 mm = _____ cm	79.6 cm = _____ m	61 m = _____ km
6. 8,542 m = _____ km	3,128 mm = _____ m	930 cm = _____ m

Metric Mass

The **gram** (g) is the basic unit of mass. The gram is used to measure very light objects. A dime equals about 2 grams.

The **kilogram** (kg) is one thousand grams. It is used to measure heavier objects. Use kg to measure a bicycle. Remember, *kilo* means 1,000.

1 kg = 1,000 g
1 g = 0.001 kg

Find: 8.4 kg = _____ g

> To change larger units to smaller units, multiply.
>
> $$1 \text{ kg} = 1,000 \text{ g}$$
> $$8.4 \times 1,000 = 8,400$$
> $$8.4 \text{ kg} = 8,400 \text{ g}$$

Find: 24.7 g = _____ kg

> To change smaller units to larger units, divide.
>
> $$1,000 \text{ g} = 1 \text{ kg}$$
> $$24.7 \div 1,000 = 0.0247$$
> $$24.7 \text{ g} = 0.0247 \text{ kg}$$

Circle the best measurement.

a   b

1. mass of a large dog   mass of a package of frozen vegetables
   27 g   27 kg   283 g   28.3 kg

2. mass of a bagel   mass of a television
   70 g   7 kg   450 g   45 kg

Change each measurement to the smaller unit.

a   b   c

3. 32 kg = _____ g   0.007 kg = _____ g   1.8 kg = _____ g

4. 0.49 kg = _____ g   825 kg = _____ g   6.783 kg = _____ g

Change each measurement to the larger unit.

a   b   c

5. 12.8 g = _____ kg   9 g = _____ kg   137 g = _____ kg

6. 5,268 g = _____ kg   25 g = _____ kg   4.9 g = _____ kg

Metric Capacity

The **liter** (L) is the basic metric unit of capacity. A liter of liquid will fill a box 10 centimeters on each side. A large jug of apple cider holds about 4 L.

A **milliliter** (mL) is one thousandth of a liter. It is used to measure very small amounts of liquid. A milliliter of liquid will fill a box 1 centimeter on each side. A small carton of milk holds about 250 mL.

Remember, *milli* **means 0.001.**

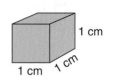

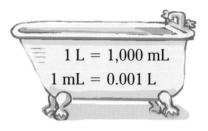

1 L = 1,000 mL
1 mL = 0.001 L

Find: 2.5 L = _____ mL

To change larger units to smaller units, multiply.

1 L = 1,000 mL

2.5 × 1,000 = 2,500

2.5 L = 2,500 mL

Find: 5,672 mL = _____ L

To change smaller units to larger units, divide.

1,000 mL = 1 L

5,672 ÷ 1,000 = 5.672

5,672 mL = 5.672 L

Circle the best measurement.

a

1. capacity of a container of yogurt
200 mL   200 L

b

capacity of a can of tomato juice
450 mL   450 L

2. capacity of a bathtub
50 mL   50 L

capacity of a large carton of juice
2.84 mL   2.84 L

Change each measurement to the smaller unit.

a

3. 27 L = _____ mL

b

5.3 L = _____ mL

c

7.45 L = _____ mL

4. 0.825 L = _____ mL

2 L = _____ mL

39.6 L = _____ mL

Change each measurement to the larger unit.

a

5. 3,096 mL = _____ L

b

6,000 mL = _____ L

c

412.5 mL = _____ L

6. 58 mL = _____ L

798 mL = _____ L

19.2 mL = _____ L

Computing Metric Measures

You can add, subtract, multiply, and divide measures that are given in two units.
For example, 2 m 26 cm uses 2 units to measure one length.

Find: 2 km 750 m + 1 km 300 m

Add.	Regroup.
2 km 750 m +1 km 300 m $\overline{}$ *3 km 1,050 m =*	**Think:** *1,050 m = 1 km 50 m* *4 km 50 m*

Find: 3 × 2 L 425 mL

Multiply.	Regroup.
2 L 425 mL × 3 $\overline{}$ *6 L 1,275 mL =*	**Think:** *1,275 mL = 1 L 275 mL* *7 L 275 mL*

Find: 4 kg 200 g − 1 kg 900 g

Subtract. You cannot subtract 900 g from 200 g.	Regroup. Then subtract. **Think:** *4 kg = 3 kg 1,000 g*
4 kg 200 g → −1 kg 900 g →	*3 kg 1,200 g* *−1 kg 900 g* $\overline{}$ *2 kg 300 g*

Find: 6 L 500 mL ÷ 5

Divide the liters.	Regroup. Divide the milliliters.
1 L 300 mL 5)6 L 500 mL *−5* ↓ $\overline{}$ *1 L 500 mL* →	*300 mL* 5)1,500 mL *1,500* $\overline{}$ *0*
Think: *1 L 500 mL = 1,500 mL*	

Find each answer. Simplify.

	a	*b*	*c*
1.	19 cm 2 mm +15 cm 29 mm $\overline{}$ *34 cm 31 mm = 37 cm 1 mm*	3 kg 750 g +4 kg 375 g	8 L 125 mL +3 L 650 mL
2.	8 kg 150 g −6 kg 200 g	5 L 425 mL −2 L 300 mL	33 m 65 cm −10 m 70 cm
3.	9 km 375 m × 3	5 kg 30 g × 7	7 L 750 mL × 6
4.	4)5 kg 100 g	5)19 L 200 mL	2)4 km 500 m

103

Problem-Solving Method: Make an Organized List

Every metric measurement has a **prefix** and a **base unit**. The prefix deca means 10. The prefix mega means 1,000,000. A **decagon** is a polygon with 10 sides, and a **megaton** is 1,000,000 tons. How many different metric measurements can you write with these two prefixes and the base units meter, liter, and gram?

Understand the problem.

- **What do you want to know?**
  how many different metric measurements you can write with those prefixes and base units

- **What information is given?**
  Prefixes: deca and mega
  Base Units: meter, liter, and gram

Plan how to solve it.

- **What method can you use?**
  You can make a list of the different prefix–base unit combinations. Then count the combinations.

Solve it.

- **How can you use this method to solve the problem?**
  Start with the first prefix and list all of its bases.
  Then do the same thing for the other prefix.

Prefix	Base	Measurement
deca-	meter	decameter
	liter	decaliter
	gram	decagram
mega-	meter	megameter
	liter	megaliter
	gram	megagram

- **What is the answer?**
  You can write 6 different metric measurements.

Look back and check your answer.

- **Is your answer reasonable?**
  You can multiply to check your answer.

  number of prefixes × number of bases = number of combinations

  $2 \times 3 = 6$

  The product matches the count.
  The answer is reasonable.

Make an organized list to solve each problem.

1. The prefix *hecto* means 100. The prefix *deci* means $\frac{1}{10}$. What are the possible measurements with these prefixes and the base units meter and gram?

    Answer _____

    _____

    _____

    _____

2. There are three main trails at the park. One is 1.2 km, one is 2.5 km, and the third is 4 km long. You can hike, bike, or ride a horse. How many different ways can you explore the trails?

    Answer _____

3. Sam, Tim, and Chantall all want to sit next to each other at the movies. In how many different ways can they do this?

    Answer _____

Change each measurement to the smaller unit.

a	*b*	*c*
1. $4\frac{1}{3}$ yd. = _____ ft.	21 cm = _____ mm	$2\frac{1}{6}$ yd. = _____ in.
2. $1\frac{1}{5}$ T. = _____ lb.	$4\frac{1}{2}$ kg = _____ g	$2\frac{1}{2}$ lb. = _____ oz.
3. $5\frac{1}{4}$ gal. = _____ pt.	21 L = _____ mL	7 qt. = _____ c.

Circle the best measurement.

a	*b*
4. distance from Miami to Atlanta	length of a desk
30 m 300 km	2.5 m 250 mm
5. mass of a pencil	capacity of a bottle
2 kg 2 g	3 L 3 mL

Change each measurement to the larger unit.

a	*b*	*c*
6. 168 oz. = _____ lb.	3,520 yd. = _____ mi.	1,123 m = _____ km
7. 5.9 g = _____ kg	4,000 lb. = _____ T.	2,102 g = _____ kg
8. 2,500 mL = _____ L	56 c. = _____ gal.	21.5 mL = _____ L

Compare. Write <, >, or =.

a	*b*
9. 36 in. _____ 4 ft.	3 km _____ 30,000 m
10. 128 oz. _____ 10 lb.	12 gal. _____ 40 c.

Find each answer.

a	*b*	*c*	*d*
11. 7 gal. 3 qt.	$3\overline{)5\,\text{cm}\,7\,\text{mm}}$	3 L 6 mL	16 gal. 5 pt.
-4 gal. 2 qt.		$-\,2$ L 2 mL	$\times$ 6

Make an organized list to solve each problem.

12. Matt has $0.75 in United States coins. He has exactly 1 half-dollar and no pennies. What are all the possible coin combinations Matt could have?

13. There are four marbles in a bag. One is black, one is silver, one is clear, and one is blue. You reach inside without looking and choose 2 marbles. What are all the possible marble pairs you could pick?

Answer _____

Answer _____

14. Sam packed black pants, jeans, and khaki pants for his vacation. He packed three different T-shirts: blue, white, and black. How many different outfits can he wear?

Answer _____

Points, Lines, and Planes

A **point** is an exact location in space.	P •	point *P* or *P*
A **plane** is a flat surface that extends forever in all directions. It is named by any three points.	*L* *M* *N* *O*	plane *LMN*
A **line** is an endless straight path.	← *A* *B* →	line *AB* or line *BA* $\overleftrightarrow{AB}$ or $\overleftrightarrow{BA}$
A **line segment** is a straight path between two points.	*R* *S*	line segment *RS* or line segment *SR* $\overline{RS}$ or $\overline{SR}$
A **ray** is an endless straight path starting at one point.	*B* *G* →	ray *BG* $\overrightarrow{BG}$

Within a plane, lines can have different relationships.

Lines that cross at one point are **intersecting lines.**

Lines that intersect to form four 90° angles are **perpendicular lines.**

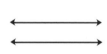

Lines that never intersect are **parallel lines.** They are always the same distance apart.

Use the drawing at right for Exercises 1–8.

1. Name a plane. _____ *plane PQR* _____

2. Name a line. _____

3. Name a line segment. _____

4. Name a ray. _____

5. Name a point. _____

6. Name 2 parallel lines. _____

7. Name 2 intersecting lines. _____

8. Name 2 perpendicular lines. _____

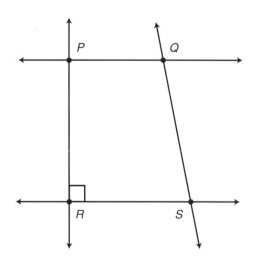

Name each figure. Write *point, plane, line, line segment,* or *ray*.

	a	b	c	d

9.

   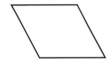   

_____ *line* _____   _____   _____   _____

Name each figure using symbols.

	a	b	c	d

10.

A

B

B

L

M

R

S

_____ $\overline{AB}$ *or* $\overline{BA}$ _____   _____   _____   _____

Describe the lines. Write *intersecting, perpendicular,* or *parallel*.

	a	b	c	d

11.

_____ *intersecting* _____   _____   _____   _____

Angles

An **angle** is two rays with a common endpoint called a **vertex**.

Angles are measured in **degrees** (°).

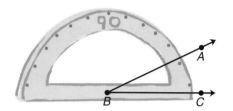

angle *ABC* or angle *CBA*
or angle *B*

∠*ABC* or ∠*CBA* or ∠*B*

Angles are classified by their size.

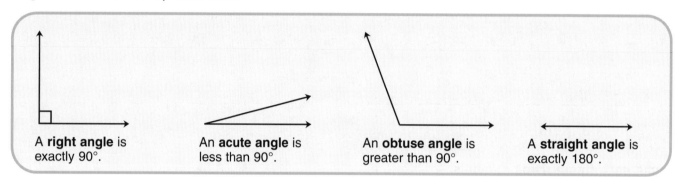

A **right angle** is exactly 90°.

An **acute angle** is less than 90°.

An **obtuse angle** is greater than 90°.

A **straight angle** is exactly 180°.

Name each angle using symbols.

a	*b*	*c*	*d*

1.

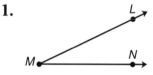

∠LMN or ∠NML _____ _____ _____

Classify each angle. Write *right, acute, obtuse,* or *straight*.

a	*b*	*c*	*d*

2.

___obtuse___ _____ _____ _____

Congruent Segments and Angles

Congruent line segments and angles have the same measure. The symbol for congruent is ≅.

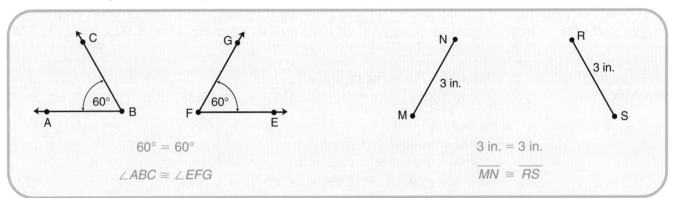

$60° = 60°$

$\angle ABC \cong \angle EFG$

$3\text{ in.} = 3\text{ in.}$

$\overline{MN} \cong \overline{RS}$

Write whether the angles are *congruent* or *not congruent*.

a

b

1.

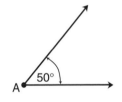

_____ *not congruent* _____

_____

Write whether the line segments are *congruent* or *not congruent*.

a

b

2.

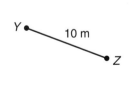

_____

_____

111

Problem-Solving Method: Make a Drawing

Madison Drive and Jefferson Drive are parallel streets in Washington, D.C. Madison runs along the north side of the park and Jefferson runs along the south of the park. 14th Street intersects both streets and is perpendicular to both streets. If you are walking west on Jefferson Drive and want to get to Madison Drive, should you turn right or left onto 14th Street?

Understand the problem.

- **What do you want to know?**
  if you should turn right or left onto 14th Street to get to Madison Drive

- **What information is given?**
  the description and directions of 3 streets in Washington, D.C.
  You are walking west on Jefferson Drive.

Plan how to solve it.

- **What method can you use?**
  You can make a drawing of the streets.

Solve it.

- **How can you use this method to solve the problem?**
  Draw and label the streets. Then follow the information in the problem to find Madison Drive from 14th Street.

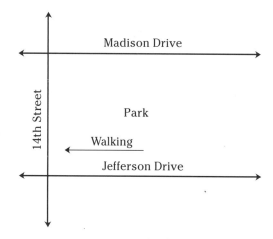

- **What is the answer?**
  You should turn right onto 14th Street.

Look back and check your answer.

- **Is your answer reasonable?**
  Reread the descriptions in the problem and check that they match your drawing.

  The answer matches the descriptions. It is reasonable.

Make a drawing to solve each problem.

1. Main Street runs east to west. Elm Street is perpendicular to and intersects Main Street. Taylor Avenue intersects both Main and Elm Streets at different points. What shape do the three streets form?

2. The town square has a statue at each corner. A bricked sidewalk starts at each statue and runs diagonally across the square. What kind of angles are formed by the intersection of the 4 sidewalks?

Answer _____

Answer _____

3. Peter and Marcia are building a stone wall that will be 38 feet long. Peter starts from one end and builds 9 feet of the wall. Marcia starts at the other end and builds 7 feet of the wall. How much of the wall is not built?

Answer _____

Perimeter of a Rectangle

Perimeter is the distance around a figure. To find the perimeter of a rectangle, count the number of units around the rectangle.

Find the perimeter of this rectangle by counting units.

Start at point *A*. Move clockwise and count the units from *A* to *B* (8), to *C* (13), to *D* (21), to *A* (26).

The perimeter of this rectangle is 26 units.

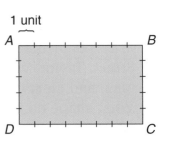

Find the perimeter of each rectangle.

a	b	c

1.

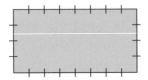

_____*16 units*_____   _____   _____

2.

    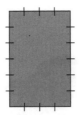   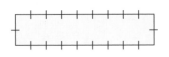

_____   _____   _____

3.

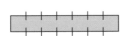      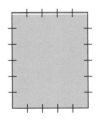

_____   _____   _____

4.

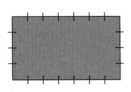

_____   _____   _____

Formula for Perimeter of a Rectangle

To find the perimeter of a rectangle, you can also use a **formula**.

Notice that the opposite sides of a rectangle are equal.

The formula, $P = 2l + 2w$, means the perimeter of a rectangle equals 2 times the length *(l)* plus 2 times the width *(w)*.

Find the perimeter of this chalkboard by using the formula.

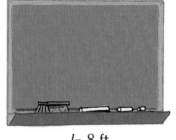

w= 5 ft.

Write the formula. $P = 2l + 2w$
Substitute the data. $P = (2 \times 8) + (2 \times 5)$
Solve the problem. $P = 16 + 10$
                          $P = 26$

The perimeter of this chalkboard is 26 feet.

l= 8 ft.

Find the perimeter of each rectangle by using the formula.

a	*b*	*c*
1. length = 15 in.	length = 32 cm	width = 2 m
width = 12 in.	width = 27 cm	length = 2.5 m
$P = 2l + 2w$		
$P = (2 \times 15) + (2 \times 12)$		
$P = 30 + 24$		
$P = 54$ in.		

2. width = 29 yd.	length = 24 in.	length = $6\frac{1}{4}$ ft.
length = 33 yd.	width = 18 in.	width = $4\frac{1}{2}$ ft.

3. length = 12.4 m	width = 46 mm	length = 22 yd.
width = 10.5 m	length = 54 mm	width = 18 yd.

4. length = 92 cm	width = 15.2 m	length = 29 ft.
width = 75 cm	length = 18.6 m	width = 27 ft.

Area of a Rectangle

Area is the number of **square units** needed to cover a figure. To find the area of a rectangle, count the number of square units covering the rectangle.

1 square unit

Find the area of this window by counting all the square units covering it.

The area of this window is 40 square units.

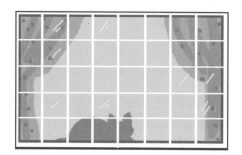

Find the area of each rectangle by counting the square units.

                  a   *b*   *c*

1.

12 square units

2.

3.

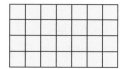   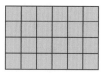

4.

Formula for Area of a Rectangle

To find the area of a rectangle, you can also use a formula.

The formula, $A = lw$, means the area of a rectangle equals the length times the width.

Find the area of the side of the doghouse by using the formula.

w= 5 ft.

Write the formula. $A = l \times w$
Substitute the data. $A = 8 \times 5$
Solve the problem. $A = 40$

The area of the side of the doghouse is 40 square feet.

Remember, write your answer in *square* units.

l= 8 ft.

Find the area of each rectangle by using the formula.

	a	b	c

1. length = 18 cm

   width = 15 cm

   $A = l \times w$
   $A = 18 \times 15$
   $A = 270$ square centimeters

length = 78 mm

width = 42 mm

_____

length = $7\frac{1}{2}$ ft.

width = $1\frac{1}{2}$ ft.

_____

2. width = 3.8 m
   length = 6.5 m

length = 19 yd.
width = 4 yd.

width = 8 ft.
length = 20 ft.

_____   _____   _____

3. length = 85 in.
   width = 37 in.

width = 1.8 m
length = 2.2 m

length = 17.5 cm
width = 4.3 cm

_____   _____   _____

4. length = $4\frac{1}{2}$ yd.
   width = $2\frac{1}{4}$ yd.

width = 9 m
length = 13 m

length = 8 in.
width = $3\frac{1}{2}$ in.

_____   _____   _____

Volume of a Rectangular Solid

Volume is the number of **cubic units** needed to fill a solid figure. To find the volume of a rectangular solid, count the number of cubic units in the rectangular box.

1 cubic unit

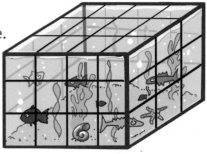

Find the volume of this aquarium by counting cubic units.

Count the number of cubes in the top layer.
Count the number of layers. Then multiply.

The volume of this aquarium is 36 cubic units.

$$\begin{array}{r} 12 \\ \times\ 3 \\ \hline 36 \end{array}$$

Find the volume of each rectangular solid by counting the cubic units.

	a	b	c

1.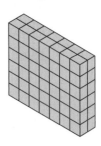

_____24 cubic units_____   _____   _____

2.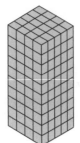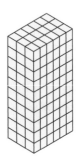

_____   _____   _____

3.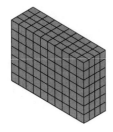

_____   _____   _____

Formula for Volume of a Rectangular Solid

To find the volume of a rectangular solid, you can also use a formula.

The formula, $V = lwh$, means the volume of a rectangular solid equals the length times the width times the height.

Find the volume of this gift box.

$l = 4$ cm
$w = 3$ cm
$h = 3$ cm

Write the formula. $V = l \times w \times h$
Substitute the data. $V = 4 \times 3 \times 3$
Solve the problem. $V = 36$

The volume of this gift box is 36 cubic centimeters.

Remember, write your answer in *cubic* units.

Find the volume of each rectangular solid. Use the formula.

a	b	c

1. length = 20 ft.
   width = 10 ft.
   height = 7 ft.

   $V = l \times w \times h$
   $V = 20 \times 10 \times 7$
   $V = 1,400$ cubic ft.

length = 25 mm
width = 24 mm
height = 10 mm

length = 34 in.
width = 28 in.
height = 16 in.

2. length = 4 cm
   width = 1.5 cm
   height = 2.6 cm

length = $12\frac{1}{2}$ in.
width = 5 in.
height = 20 in.

length = 15 ft.
width = 12 ft.
height = 8 ft.

3. length = 20 yd.
   width = 16 yd.
   height = 6 yd.

length = 8 m
width = 5.5 m
height = 6.4 m

length = 12 yd.
width = $8\frac{1}{4}$ yd.
height = 10 yd.

Problem-Solving Method: Use a Formula

One of the world's largest chocolate candy bars was made in England. It was 12.9 feet long, 4.9 feet wide, and 1 foot tall. How many cubic feet of chocolate were used to make the bar?

Understand the problem.

- **What do you want to know?**
  how much chocolate was in the candy bar

- **What information is given?**
  The bar was 12.9 feet long, 4.9 feet wide, and 1 foot tall.

Plan how to solve it.

- **What method can you use?**
  You can use a formula.

Solve it.

- **How can you use this method to solve the problem?**
  Since a bar is a rectangular solid, you can use the formula for the volume of a rectangular solid.

$$V = l \times w \times h$$
$$V = 12.9 \times 4.9 \times 1$$
$$V = 63.21$$

- **What is the answer?**
  The bar had 63.21 cubic feet of chocolate.

Look back and check your answer.

- **Is your answer reasonable?**
  You can estimate to check your answer.

  $10 \times 5 \times 1 = 50$

  The estimate is close to the answer.
  The answer is reasonable.

Use a formula to solve each problem.

1. The total capacity of your lungs is about the same as the volume of a 12 in. × 8 in. × 5 in. shoe box. About how many cubic inches of air can your lungs hold?

Answer _____

2. A regulation football field is 100 yards long and $53\frac{1}{3}$ yards wide. How many square yards of grass would you need to cover the whole field?

Answer _____

3. Greg's rectangular fish tank is 30.5 cm long, 18.6 cm wide, and 12 cm tall. How many cubic centimeters of water will fill Greg's fish tank?

Answer _____

4. A twin bed is 39 inches wide and 72 inches long. How long is a dust ruffle that goes around the bottom of a twin bed?

Answer _____

5. A professional soccer field is 75 meters wide and 110 meters long. Linda ran around the soccer field three times after practice. How far did she run?

Answer _____

6. Each can of paint covers 40 square feet. Each wall in Charlene's bedroom is 10 feet tall and 8 feet wide. How many cans does she need to paint the 4 walls?

Answer _____

Use the drawing at right for Exercises 1–7.

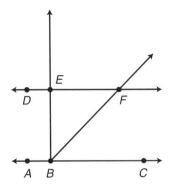

1. Name a point. _____

2. Name a line. _____

3. Name an acute angle. _____

4. Name a ray. _____

5. Name a pair of parallel lines. _____

6. Name a line segment. _____

7. Name two congruent angles. _____

Count the units to find the following.

                                     a   b   c

8.

Perimeter _____   Area _____   Volume _____

Find the perimeter of each rectangle. Use the formula $P = 2l + 2w$.

        a   b   c

9. length = 2.7 m   length = 90 cm   length = $11\frac{2}{3}$ yd.

    width = 1.4 m   width = 80 cm   width = $5\frac{2}{3}$ yd.

_____   _____   _____

Find the area of each rectangle. Use the formula $A = l \times w$.

        a   b   c

10. length = 21 mm   length = $42\frac{1}{2}$ in.   length = 3.9 cm

    width = 8 mm   width = $30\frac{1}{2}$ in.   width = 1.7 cm

_____   _____   _____

Find the volume of each rectangle. Use the formula $V = l \times w \times h$.

        a   b   c

11. length = 8 yd.   length = 10 m   length = 25 ft.

    width = 6 yd.   width = 3.4 m   width = $2\frac{1}{4}$ ft.

    height = 9 yd.   height = 5 m   height = 4 ft.

_____   _____   _____

Make a drawing to solve each problem.

12. Lombard and Pratt Streets both run east to west and are parallel to each other. Charles and Franklin Streets both run north to south and are parallel to each other. Describe the shape that is formed where the four streets meet.

Answer _____

13. Karen, Tremont, Joe, and Anita sat on the same side of the picnic table. Karen sat between Joe and Tremont. Joe sat between Anita and Karen. Which two people sat at the ends of the table?

Answer _____

Use a formula to solve each problem.

14. In 1506, Leonardo da Vinci painted the *Mona Lisa* on a piece of pinewood, 30 in. by $20\frac{7}{8}$ in. How much wood was needed to frame the *Mona Lisa?*

Answer _____

15. A compact disc case is 14 cm long, 12.5 cm wide, and 1 cm tall. What is the area of the case's top cover? What is the volume of the case?

Answer _____

Answer Key

Page 6

1.

	4	6	8,	9	3	7,	5	7	4
5,	9	1	0,	3	8	2,	6	5	4
			8,	3	4	2,	3	8	4
				7	6,	0	9	8	

	a	b
5.	ten thousands	hundreds
6.	ones	hundred thousands
7.	tens	billions
8.	thousands	hundred millions

9. one hundred thirty-two thousand, three hundred forty-two
10. seven million, six hundred forty-two thousand, three hundred fifty-three

Page 7

	a	b
1.	<	>
2.	<	<
3.	<	=
4.	<	>
5.	<	<
6.	<	>
7.	<	>

	a	b	c
8.	21	54	96
9.	468	487	532
10.	231	322	632
11.	45,875	67,956	94,234
12.	543,865	565,978	765,645
13.	13,764	16,576	432,877

Page 8

	a	b	c	d
1.	1,011	1,128	1,080	1,159
2.	14,867	102,038	82,385	1,290,838
3.	1,100,178	168,317	1,251,129	903,320
4.	12,299	1,071		
5.	307,877	4,693		

Page 9

	a	b	c	d
1.	1,348	1,611	717	1,225
2.	1,071	1,292	4,872	11,705
3.	2,293,094	162,442	2,358,875	2,809,623
4.	1,478		1,709	

Page 10

	a	b	c	d
1.	289	198	6	149
2.	354	154	4,101	2,735
3.	5,564	20,168	205,145	677,112
4.	511	177		
5.	10,968	2,467		

Page 11

	a	b	c	d
1.	7,200	5,100	53,800	539,000
2.	11,000	12,000	15,000	19,000
3.	300	500	200	100
4.	53,000	13,000	70,000	42,000

Page 13

1. Aaron is 11 years old.
Laura is 12 years old.
2. *Titanic* won 11 awards.
Gone with the Wind won 8 awards.
3. 16 legs
4. Yoga was 50 minutes.
Aerobics was 20 minutes.
5. 6 dimes, 1 penny or 1 quarter, 2 dimes, 3 nickels, and 1 penny

Page 14

	a	b	c	d
1.	360	39	216	175
2.	870	1,803	5,348	7,536
3.	19,278	24,000	31,824	41,670
4.	81,779	257,050	70,028	1,211,105
5.	1,719	235,564	1,698,429	

Page 15

	a	b	c	d
1.	880	4,560	4,410	5,040
2.	1,200	4,200	17,400	200,300
3.	30,100	222,300	240,000	

Page 16

	a	b	c	d
1.	112,993	228,046	194,181	562,890
2.	572,850	362,043	731,620	321,200
3.	267,786	280,500	431,844	

Page 17

	a	b	c	d
1.	1,500	1,000	4,200	8,100
2.	1,400	1,500	2,400	4,800
3.	15,000	63,000	27,000	70,000
4.	1,400	4,500	21,000	

Page 18

	a	b	c	d
1.	34 R1	94 R4	96 R1	54 R4
2.	167 R12	70 R54	127 R12	140 R14
3.	153 R2	156 R4	2724 R4	

Page 19

	a	b	c	d
1.	11 R39	5 R30	18 R8	49 R7
2.	127 R10	192 R16	147 R20	98 R10
3.	55 R25	259 R3		

Page 20

	a	b
1.	too large; 1	too small; 4
2.	too large; 3	too large; 2
3.	too large; 7	too large; 2

Page 21

	a	b	c	d
1.	304	107	205	209
2.	507	602	208	

Page 22

	a	b	c
1.	40	70	90
2.	700	300	600
3.	40	20	20
4.	20	15	8

Page 24

1. addition;
147,825 sq. mi.
2. subtraction;
13,600 people
3. division;
7 hours
4. division;
$13 an hour
5. division; 15 feet

Page 25

	a	b
1.	millions	ten thousands
2.	1,050,045	
3.	2,007,006	

	a	b	c
4.	>	<	<
5.	702	720	722
6.	6,789	9,786	9,789
7.	563	387	23,826
8.	331,889	187,042	296,402
9.	610	200	1,000
10.	110,000	20,000	27,000

Page 26

	a	b	c	d
11.	138	188	2,064	4,984
12.	11,700	47,775	290,496	1,743,200
13.	1,856,960	386,078	332,906	450,000
14.	84 R3	222 R2	1,275 R3	13,409
15.	22 R10	9 R33	219 R6	120 R2
16.	2,543 R3	782 R2	704 R76	1,509 R39
17.	4,800	50	1,600	
18.	800	35,000	4	

Page 27

19. Shawn made 48 cupcakes. Andy made 38 cupcakes.
20. 1 nickel, 3 pennies 3 quarters, 1 dime
21. addition; 802 cards
22. multiplication; 114,500 papers
23. subtraction; 1,153 cars

Page 28

	a	b	c
1.	$\frac{2}{3}$ or two-thirds	$\frac{5}{8}$ or five-eighths	$\frac{1}{5}$ or one-fifth
2.	$\frac{2}{6}$ or two-sixths	$\frac{7}{10}$ or seven-tenths	$\frac{3}{7}$ or three-sevenths
3.	$\frac{3}{8}$	$\frac{1}{4}$	$\frac{4}{5}$
4.	five-sixths	two-sevenths	seven-eighths

Page 29

	a	b	c	d
1.	4	3	7	8
2.	$3\frac{3}{4}$	$4\frac{1}{5}$	$3\frac{5}{6}$	$3\frac{1}{2}$
3.	$\frac{27}{10}$	$\frac{25}{3}$	$\frac{31}{6}$	$\frac{17}{5}$

Page 30

	a	b	c	d
1.	10	12	8	4
2.	15	6	20	14
3.	$\frac{2}{6}$	$\frac{5}{10}$	$\frac{14}{20}$	$\frac{14}{21}$
	$\frac{3}{6}$	$\frac{6}{10}$	$\frac{15}{20}$	$\frac{15}{21}$

Page 31

	a	b	c	d
1.	$\frac{3}{7}$	$\frac{1}{5}$	$\frac{1}{3}$	$\frac{2}{3}$
2.	$\frac{2}{3}$	$\frac{1}{4}$	$\frac{2}{5}$	$\frac{5}{6}$
3.	1	$\frac{3}{5}$	$\frac{1}{6}$	$\frac{3}{7}$
4.	$\frac{3}{4}$	$\frac{1}{3}$	$\frac{1}{2}$	$\frac{3}{4}$
5.	$\frac{3}{7}$	$\frac{1}{10}$	$\frac{1}{9}$	$\frac{1}{2}$

Page 32

	a	b	c	d	e
1.	$\frac{1}{2}$	$\frac{2}{5}$	$\frac{1}{2}$	$\frac{3}{8}$	$\frac{5}{8}$
2.	$1\frac{1}{6}$	$1\frac{1}{2}$	$1\frac{3}{10}$	$1\frac{2}{5}$	$1\frac{5}{12}$
3.	$\frac{1}{4}$	$\frac{2}{5}$	$\frac{1}{6}$	$\frac{1}{2}$	$\frac{3}{4}$

Page 33

	a	b	c	d
1.	$\frac{3}{10}$	$\frac{3}{4}$	$\frac{7}{8}$	$\frac{7}{8}$
2.	$\frac{5}{6}$	$\frac{2}{3}$	$\frac{3}{5}$	$\frac{2}{3}$
3.	$\frac{4}{5}$	$\frac{9}{16}$	$\frac{11}{12}$	$\frac{7}{9}$
4.	$\frac{5}{9}$	$\frac{7}{24}$	$\frac{11}{18}$	

Page 34

	a	b	c	d
1.	$1\frac{1}{6}$	$\frac{13}{14}$	$1\frac{5}{12}$	$1\frac{8}{45}$
2.	$1\frac{13}{24}$	$1\frac{5}{24}$	$1\frac{7}{15}$	$\frac{20}{21}$
3.	$1\frac{7}{12}$	$\frac{19}{30}$	$1\frac{13}{30}$	$1\frac{1}{18}$
4.	$\frac{19}{28}$	$1\frac{24}{55}$	$\frac{11}{28}$	

Page 35

1. JAMAL'S CD COLLECTION

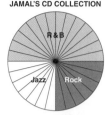

2. FAVORITE ICE CREAM

3. LAURA'S WORKDAY

4. HAIR COLOR IN UNITED STATES

Page 37

	a	b	c	d
1.	$4\frac{3}{4}$	$8\frac{5}{8}$	$6\frac{3}{8}$	$9\frac{7}{8}$
2.	$21\frac{1}{2}$	$17\frac{3}{5}$	$19\frac{3}{10}$	$14\frac{4}{9}$
3.	$2\frac{7}{12}$	$3\frac{11}{12}$	$7\frac{5}{6}$	$1\frac{29}{56}$
4.	$11\frac{7}{24}$	$17\frac{7}{12}$	$11\frac{9}{10}$	$15\frac{4}{5}$

Page 38

	a	b	c	d
1.	$5\frac{1}{3}$	$10\frac{7}{30}$	$4\frac{5}{9}$	$7\frac{17}{56}$
2.	$10\frac{7}{12}$	$14\frac{1}{9}$	$18\frac{41}{77}$	$11\frac{5}{12}$
3.	$10\frac{5}{12}$	$7\frac{5}{6}$	$11\frac{3}{10}$	$9\frac{1}{6}$
4.	$13\frac{7}{12}$	$18\frac{3}{5}$	$19\frac{7}{10}$	$10\frac{1}{2}$

Page 39

	a	b	c	d
1.	$4; 3; \frac{1}{12}$	$5; 4; \frac{1}{20}$	$6; 5; \frac{1}{10}$	$4; 3; \frac{1}{6}$
2.	$\frac{7}{12}$	$\frac{11}{24}$	$\frac{3}{10}$	$\frac{3}{10}$

3. $\frac{1}{2}$ $\frac{5}{18}$ $\frac{3}{8}$ $\frac{19}{36}$

4. $\frac{3}{5}$ $\frac{37}{72}$ $\frac{13}{24}$

Page 40

	a	b	c	d
1.	$4; 7\frac{4}{4}$	$3; 11\frac{3}{3}$	$8; 17\frac{8}{8}$	$12; 27\frac{12}{12}$
2.	$3\frac{1}{3}$	$4; 1\frac{1}{4}$	$8; 3\frac{3}{8}$	$6; 4\frac{1}{6}$
3.	$2\frac{1}{2}$	$4\frac{3}{8}$	$3\frac{4}{5}$	$14\frac{7}{10}$
4.	$2\frac{5}{6}$	$15\frac{1}{4}$	$2\frac{4}{9}$	$8\frac{2}{5}$

Page 41

	a	b	c
1.	$5\frac{2}{5}$	$6\frac{1}{2}$	$3\frac{2}{3}$
2.	$8\frac{3}{8}$	$1\frac{2}{3}$	$2\frac{23}{40}$
3.	$6\frac{1}{6}$	$11\frac{9}{10}$	$8\frac{1}{8}$
4.	$1\frac{7}{10}$	$1\frac{23}{28}$	$14\frac{2}{3}$

Page 43

1. no   **2.** yes
3. no   **4.** about 6 inches
5. no

Page 44

	a	b	c	
1.	$\frac{1}{3}$ or one-third	$\frac{4}{6}$ or four-sixths	$\frac{6}{7}$ or six-sevenths	

	a	b	c	d
2.	7	$8\frac{2}{3}$	5	$3\frac{1}{2}$
3.	$\frac{13}{4}$	$\frac{23}{8}$	$\frac{23}{5}$	$\frac{17}{10}$
4.	12	5	16	15
5.	$\frac{3}{12}$ $\frac{4}{12}$	$\frac{4}{20}$ $\frac{15}{20}$	$\frac{9}{24}$ $\frac{16}{24}$	$\frac{11}{22}$ $\frac{8}{22}$
6.	$\frac{1}{6}$	$\frac{1}{3}$	$\frac{1}{15}$	$\frac{1}{3}$
7.	$\frac{1}{7}$	$\frac{3}{5}$	$\frac{1}{9}$	$\frac{1}{2}$

Page 45

	a	b	c	d
8.	$1\frac{1}{7}$	$\frac{7}{9}$	$3\frac{3}{11}$	$5\frac{23}{40}$
9.	$8\frac{8}{9}$	$7\frac{7}{24}$	$5\frac{7}{10}$	$\frac{19}{42}$
10.	$1\frac{7}{12}$	$15\frac{19}{21}$	$6\frac{4}{11}$	$4\frac{9}{16}$
11.	$6\frac{1}{2}$	$21\frac{7}{9}$	$28\frac{1}{12}$	$12\frac{27}{40}$
12.	$\frac{7}{24}$	$5\frac{3}{5}$	$2\frac{4}{7}$	$2\frac{3}{4}$
13.	$\frac{1}{2}$	$1\frac{1}{12}$	$\frac{1}{4}$	$\frac{7}{12}$
14.	$4\frac{25}{36}$	$\frac{3}{10}$	$6\frac{11}{24}$	$1\frac{1}{2}$
15.	$2\frac{7}{20}$	$3\frac{6}{7}$	$3\frac{13}{15}$	$\frac{8}{99}$

Page 46

	a	b
1.	$\frac{2}{15}$	$\frac{3}{50}$
2.	$\frac{12}{35}$	$\frac{35}{48}$
3.	$\frac{2}{7}$	$\frac{2}{11}$
4.	$\frac{1}{4}$	$\frac{3}{16}$

5. $\frac{1}{8}$ $\frac{1}{12}$

Page 47

	a	b
1.	$\frac{1}{4}$	$\frac{7}{18}$
2.	$\frac{3}{14}$	$\frac{1}{16}$
3.	$\frac{1}{12}$	$\frac{1}{12}$
4.	$\frac{7}{12}$	$\frac{13}{20}$
5.	$\frac{1}{4}$	$\frac{1}{6}$
6.	$\frac{1}{2}$	$\frac{1}{2}$

Page 48

	a	b	c	d	e
1.	$\frac{7}{1}$	$\frac{18}{1}$	$\frac{20}{1}$	$\frac{4}{1}$	$\frac{12}{1}$
2.	2	4	$4\frac{1}{2}$		
3.	$1\frac{1}{2}$	9	$6\frac{2}{3}$		
4.	6	$7\frac{1}{2}$	20		
5.	24	$16\frac{1}{2}$	20		

Page 49

	a	b	c
1.	15	7	36
2.	10	14	14
3.	13	21	50
4.	$66\frac{2}{3}$	$11\frac{1}{2}$	$12\frac{4}{5}$
5.	$8\frac{2}{5}$	$10\frac{1}{3}$	79
6.	$41\frac{1}{3}$	$123\frac{1}{3}$	$4\frac{8}{9}$

Page 50

	a	b	c
1.	$\frac{3}{5}$	$\frac{3}{5}$	$\frac{5}{6}$
2.	$2\frac{1}{10}$	$\frac{3}{4}$	$\frac{17}{20}$
3.	$\frac{14}{15}$	$3\frac{11}{12}$	$5\frac{2}{5}$
4.	3	$3\frac{1}{2}$	$3\frac{1}{2}$
5.	10	$\frac{1}{2}$	3

Page 51

	a	b	c
1.	$7\frac{1}{5}$	$2\frac{1}{4}$	$2\frac{2}{3}$
2.	$8\frac{1}{3}$	$16\frac{1}{4}$	$7\frac{1}{3}$
3.	$18\frac{3}{8}$	$14\frac{4}{5}$	$56\frac{1}{4}$
4.	15	9	15
5.	12	8	9

Page 53

1. 4 inches   **2.** $102.00

3. $\frac{1}{4}$ hour   **4.** pink

5. $30\frac{5}{12}$ feet   **6.** $1\frac{3}{4}$ tablespoons

Page 54

	a	b	c	d	e
1.	$\frac{3}{2}$	6	$\frac{8}{7}$	$\frac{9}{5}$	$\frac{1}{8}$
2.	$\frac{5}{3}$	$\frac{13}{9}$	$\frac{4}{7}$	$\frac{1}{25}$	4

	a	b	c	d
3.	$\frac{13}{3}, \frac{3}{13}$	$\frac{14}{5}, \frac{5}{14}$	$\frac{16}{9}, \frac{9}{16}$	$\frac{21}{4}, \frac{4}{21}$
4.	$\frac{56}{11}, \frac{11}{56}$	$\frac{21}{13}, \frac{13}{21}$	$\frac{49}{8}, \frac{8}{49}$	$\frac{23}{6}, \frac{6}{23}$
5.	$\frac{9}{7}$	$\frac{5}{1}$	$\frac{1}{9}$	$\frac{2}{7}$

Page 55

	a	b	
1.	$\frac{14}{15}$	$1\frac{1}{8}$	
2.	$1\frac{1}{2}$	$1\frac{1}{2}$	

	a	b	c
3.	8	$\frac{5}{9}$	4
4.	$\frac{9}{16}$	1	$\frac{5}{18}$
5.	3	$1\frac{5}{9}$	$1\frac{1}{10}$
6.	$1\frac{9}{16}$	$1\frac{5}{12}$	$5\frac{1}{2}$

Page 56

	a	b
1.	$\frac{1}{16}$	$\frac{1}{8}$
2.	$\frac{3}{8}$	$\frac{1}{15}$

	a	b	c
3.	$\frac{1}{21}$	$\frac{1}{30}$	$\frac{1}{48}$
4.	$\frac{1}{32}$	$\frac{1}{36}$	$\frac{1}{30}$
5.	$\frac{3}{16}$	$\frac{1}{60}$	$\frac{1}{65}$
6.	$\frac{1}{50}$	$\frac{1}{36}$	$\frac{3}{50}$

Page 57

1.	$12\frac{1}{2}$	$7\frac{1}{2}$
2.	4	$3\frac{1}{2}$
3.	14	15
4.	$3\frac{1}{5}$	30
5.	8	9
6.	$32\frac{2}{3}$	12

Page 58

	a	b	c
1.	$\frac{2}{3}$	$\frac{1}{2}$	$2\frac{1}{2}$
2.	$\frac{2}{3}$	$1\frac{2}{5}$	$\frac{3}{4}$
3.	$1\frac{1}{3}$	$\frac{5}{12}$	$\frac{3}{8}$
4.	$1\frac{1}{5}$	$\frac{5}{36}$	$\frac{2}{9}$
5.	$\frac{5}{14}$	$\frac{3}{8}$	$\frac{2}{9}$

Page 59

	a	b	c
1.	7	9	14
2.	$8\frac{5}{6}$	$14\frac{1}{2}$	$1\frac{9}{10}$
3.	46	$15\frac{3}{7}$	$2\frac{5}{8}$
4.	$8\frac{9}{14}$	$2\frac{7}{8}$	$14\frac{2}{5}$
5.	$3\frac{3}{32}$	$5\frac{4}{7}$	$6\frac{4}{7}$

Page 60

	a	b
1.	$1\frac{1}{3}$	$6\frac{2}{3}$
2.	$1\frac{1}{15}$	$5\frac{1}{3}$

3.	$1\frac{1}{5}$	$\frac{36}{65}$
4.	$3\frac{7}{51}$	$\frac{3}{10}$
5.	$\frac{2}{3}$	2
6.	$\frac{5}{6}$	$\frac{5}{12}$

Page 62

1. $9\frac{1}{2}$ pieces   2. $\frac{5}{8}$ pound
3. 6 honeybees   4. 40 magnets
5. $6\frac{13}{15}$ inches   6. $3\frac{23}{99}$ feet

Page 63

	a	b	c	d	e
1.	$\frac{19}{1}$	$\frac{3}{1}$	$\frac{25}{1}$	$\frac{16}{1}$	$\frac{17}{1}$
2.	$\frac{4}{15}$	$\frac{2}{21}$	$\frac{5}{16}$		
3.	$\frac{3}{8}$	$\frac{5}{8}$	$\frac{1}{16}$		
4.	$3\frac{3}{4}$	9	$4\frac{1}{3}$		
5.	8	$16\frac{4}{5}$	10		
6.	$13\frac{1}{3}$	42	$40\frac{4}{5}$		
7.	$3\frac{3}{4}$	$1\frac{4}{5}$	$\frac{19}{48}$		
8.	18	$11\frac{6}{35}$	$13\frac{1}{8}$		
9.	$7\frac{1}{14}$	$11\frac{11}{15}$	$28\frac{1}{3}$		

Page 64

	a	b	c	d	e
10.	$\frac{7}{1}$	$\frac{12}{5}$	$\frac{9}{4}$	$\frac{7}{17}$	$\frac{15}{2}$

	a	b	c
11.	2	3	$1\frac{1}{20}$
12.	$1\frac{5}{9}$	$\frac{5}{36}$	$2\frac{10}{11}$
13.	$\frac{13}{144}$	$\frac{5}{162}$	$\frac{2}{25}$
14.	$\frac{1}{16}$	$\frac{1}{75}$	$\frac{1}{12}$
15.	35	24	$19\frac{1}{4}$
16.	$\frac{12}{25}$	$\frac{23}{48}$	$\frac{23}{160}$
17.	$4\frac{6}{11}$	$1\frac{1}{5}$	$1\frac{53}{150}$
18.	$\frac{152}{531}$	$5\frac{5}{24}$	$2\frac{9}{10}$

Page 65

19. $4\frac{1}{3}$ jars or 4 full jars   20. $62\frac{1}{2}$ cm
21. 28 times   22. $1\frac{1}{20}$ feet
23. 30 passes

Page 66

	a	b
1.	0.2	0.02
2.	0.002	6.02
3.	0.021	1.001

4. eight and seven hundredths
5. fifty-three and nine thousandths
6. seventy-six and twelve hundredths

	a	b	c
7.	$6.00	$0.60	$0.06
8.	$0.99	$0.12	$31.00

9. $420.05
10. $3,000.98

Page 67

	a	b	c
1.	<	<	<
2.	<	>	>
3.	=	<	>

	a	b
4.	0.2 0.4 0.42	0.031 0.13 0.31
5.	0.081 0.18 8.1	2.75 27.5 275

Page 68

	a	b	c	d
1.	$\frac{5}{10}$	$\frac{4}{10}$	$\frac{2}{10}$	$\frac{6}{10}$
2.	$\frac{5}{100}$	$\frac{4}{100}$	$\frac{2}{100}$	$\frac{6}{100}$
3.	$2\frac{1}{10}$	$45\frac{9}{10}$	$31\frac{6}{10}$	$99\frac{9}{10}$
4.	$3\frac{94}{100}$	$6\frac{25}{100}$	$12\frac{54}{100}$	$10\frac{1}{100}$
5.	0.9	0.3	0.1	0.8
6.	0.07	0.91	0.063	0.527
7.	6.7	4.2	8.7	7.6
8.	2.04	6.10	1.754	3.062

Page 69

	a	b	c
1.	0.4	0.25	0.5
2.	0.25	0.2	0.35
3.	4.25	3.5	2.6
4.	1.48	2.15	3.16
5.	6.2	10.75	
6.	3.2	4.28	
7.	13.5	7.4	

Page 71

1. Chile = 9.5   2. hand = 16.42 ft.
   Russia = $9\frac{1}{10}$ face = $17\frac{1}{4}$ ft.
   Alaska = $9\frac{1}{5}$ tablet = 25.58 ft.
3. Proxima Centauri

Page 72

	a	b	c	d
1.	4	4	3	8
2.	44	52	45	73
3.	6	9	5	10
4.	$4	$25	$8	$6
5.	$8	$3	$10	$62
6.	$1	$6	$3	$9
7.	0.6	0.9	0.6	0.8
8.	4.1	8.7	2.3	9.3
9.	40	25.8	72	21.6

Page 73

	a	b	c	d
1.	41.1	89.0	47.8	$17.87
2.	11.035	8.104	21.81	38.59
3.	$77.99	$39.93	3.248	3.629
4.	58.92	321.64	7.471	91.999

Page 74

	a	b	c
1.	8	$7	$22
2.	0	$3	$50
3.	7	13	67
4.	6.4	7.2	41.7
5.	116.5	36.4	2

Page 76

1. $289.73   2. 60 years old
3. 28 students   4. 54.38 cm
5. 10 people

Page 77

	a	b
1.	0.067	0.76

2. forty-two and six hundred fifteen thousandths
3. seventy-eight thousandths
4. $68.27
5. $405.03

	a	b	c
6.	>	>	<

Column 1

	a			b		
7.	0.052	0.25	0.5	0.019	0.19	0.91

	a	b	c	d
8.	$\frac{3}{10}$	$\frac{25}{100}$ or $\frac{1}{4}$	$\frac{7}{100}$	$\frac{8}{10}$ or $\frac{4}{5}$
9.	$1\frac{75}{100}$ or $1\frac{3}{4}$	$5\frac{2}{10}$ or $5\frac{1}{5}$	$24\frac{6}{100}$ or $24\frac{3}{50}$	$16\frac{75}{100}$ or $16\frac{3}{4}$
10.	1.08	0.7	0.6	0.44
11.	2.75.6	10.25	8.75	

Page 78

	a	b	c	d
12.	8	2	4	1
13.	$8	$4	$9	$15
14.	0.4	0.2	5.1	72.1
15.	111.6	3.958	86.44	69.314
16.	$90.00	0.19	39.639	357.86
17.	14	11	79	3
18.	9.7	12.6	2.7	13.2

Page 79

19. Donovan Bailey
20. Douglas fir = 100.3 m; redwood = 83.88 m; giant sequoia = 95.4 m
21. 53.35 feet
22. $25.20

Page 80

	a	b	c
1.	5.8	58	0.58
2.	75	8.3	46
3.	280	70	7
4.	4,600	6,200	75
5.	31	310	3,150

Page 81

	a	b	c	d
1.	1.6	0.96	23.5	18.552
2.	1.28	1,139.6	10.857	0.874
3.	78.052	7.175	11.776	890.709
4.	631.4	68.8	50,232	

Page 82

	a	b	c	d
1.	0.40	0.54	3.64	3.84
2.	0.31	0.036	0.03	0.032
3.	3.336	33.06	5.1072	4.488
4.	0.00822	0.61632	2.34364	

Page 84

1. Earth ~~is 92.96 million miles from the sun~~. It orbits the sun ~~in about 365.26 days,~~ traveling at an average speed of 18.51 miles per second. How far does Earth travel in 1 minute? (60 seconds) 1,110.6 miles

2. Fleas can jump up to 150 times the length of their bodies. ~~This is equivalent to a person jumping nearly 1,000 feet~~. The average flea is about 0.2 inch long. How high can it jump? 30 inches

3. Fingernails grow about 0.004 inch a day. ~~After not cutting his nails for 44 years, a man in India has the world's longest nails. His thumbnail is 4.67 feet long.~~ How many inches do fingernails grow in 1 week? (7 days) 0.028 inch

4. ~~Every day, 274,000 carats of diamonds are mined.~~ One carat is 0.02 grams. The Cullinan Diamond is ~~the largest diamond ever discovered.~~ It is 3,106 carats. How many grams does the Cullinan Diamond weigh? 62.12 grams

5. The movie *Forrest Gump* earned a total of $679.7 million worldwide. $329.7 million of that total was made in the United

Column 2

States. ~~Forrest Gump was nominated for 13 Academy Awards and won 6.~~ How much of its total earnings were made outside the U.S.? $350 million

6. The "Rattler" ~~is one of the world's tallest wooden roller coasters. Each ride~~ is 2.25 minutes long. "Superman the Escape" is ~~one of the world's tallest steel roller coasters, at~~ 415 feet. Its ride lasts 0.467 minutes. How much longer is a ride on the "Rattler" than on "Superman"? 1.783 minutes

Page 85

	a	b	c
1.	0.689	0.07	0.056
2.	1.23	0.049	0.81
3.	0.1411	0.0003	0.0289
4.	0.037737	0.00991	0.1342
5.	0.0039	5.555	0.00715

Page 86

	a	b	c	d
1.	2.2	4.6	$0.64	1.6
2.	1.2	5.1	5.2	$0.26
3.	0.628	54.32	0.55	

Page 87

	a	b	c	d
1.	2.6	17	5.8	3.3
2.	5.4	7.6	12.6	78.1
3.	1.8	1.66	64.1	

Page 88

	a	b	c	d
1.	4	90	60	150
2.	600	2,700	3,500	1,830
3.	360	530	8,700	

Page 89

	a	b	c	d
1.	2.075	11.42	2.07	0.1095
2.	1.75	21.25	2.5	102.4

Page 90

	a	b	c
1.	6.3	7.33	0.8
2.	$0.33	$40.58	$21.00

Page 92

1. 3 / 30 / 300   **2.** 24 / 2.4 / 0.24
Answer = 300 days   Answer = 0.24 mi.

3. 2 / 20 / 200 / 2,000   **4.** 80 / 8 / 0.8 / 0.08
Answer = 2,000 mL   Answer = $0.08

5. 3 / 30 / 300   **6.** 45 / 4.5 / 0.45
Answer = 300 nickels   Answer = $0.45

Page 93

	a	b	c
1.	23.1	56	7,800
2.	8.3	640	380

	a	b	c	d
3.	14.46	30.084	$2.01	7.28
4.	3.4	2,123.8	69.825	$203.88
5.	0.45	2.52	13.44	80.01
6.	0.0854	0.0594	62.31	5.3998
7.	42.5	182.5	1,328	
8.	0.315	0.5336	4.8972	

Page 94

	a	b	c
9.	0.034	0.0092	0.00158
10.	0.005	0.019	0.006495

Column 3

	a	b	c	d
11.	1.3	6.3	$7.60	2.1
12.	1.5	22	19	26.5
13.	300	20	1,128	470
14.	1.3	$2.15	0.35	

Page 95

15. ~~Pluto is the farthest planet from the sun, at 5.9 billion kilometers.~~ It takes Pluto ~~90,950 days to~~ orbit the sun at a speed of 4.74 kilometers per second. How far does Pluto travel in 30 seconds? 142.2 km

16. In 1996, ~~31.9% of students in the United States had access to a computer~~. The average student that year used a computer 5.3 hours a week. How many hours did the average student use a computer each day in 1996? Round the answer to the nearest tenth. (1 week = 7 days) about 0.8 hour

17. ~~In-line skates were introduced to the United States in the late 1970s.~~ In 1998, the record for the highest speed on in-line skates was set at 64.02 miles per hour. How far could a person skate in 2 hours at this speed? 128.04 miles

18. ~~On December 17, 1903,~~ Orville Wright became the first man to fly an engine-powered airplane. His flight ~~took place near Kitty Hawk, North Carolina~~, and covered 120 feet in 0.2 minutes. On average, how many feet per minute did the plane fly? 600 feet/minute

19. 9 / 90 / 900   **20.** 24 / 2.4 / 0.24
Answer = 900 cups   Answer = $0.24

Page 96

	a	b	c
1.	$15\frac{1}{2}$	7,920	88
2.	45	63	7,040
3.	$4\frac{1}{4}$	$12\frac{2}{3}$	5
4.	$2\frac{1}{2}$	$18\frac{1}{2}$	3
5.	<	>	
6.	=	>	

Page 97

	a	b	c
1.	52	5,000	96
2.	8,000	22	67
3.	$3\frac{5}{16}$	$3\frac{1}{2}$	5
4.	$4\frac{1}{2}$	$2\frac{1}{4}$	$1\frac{1}{5}$
5.	=	>	
6.	>	<	

Page 98

	a	b	c
1.	17	9	26
2.	33	36	24
3.	$1\frac{3}{4}$	$2\frac{5}{8}$	$5\frac{1}{2}$
4.	6	7	$3\frac{3}{8}$
5.	>	<	
6.	=	<	

Page 99

	a	b	c
1.	8 gal 1 qt.	14 ft 2 in.	11 yd.
2.	1 yd. 2 ft.	1 gal. 3 qt.	73 lb. 8 oz.
3.	39 ft. 8 in.	1 lb. 5 oz.	1 yd. 1 ft.

Page 100

	a	b
1.	2 cm	300 km
2.	8 mm	5 m

	a	b	c
3.	14,500	725	180
4.	340	21,000	900
5.	4.8	0.796	0.061
6.	8.542	3.128	9.3

Page 101

	a	b
1.	27 kg	283 g
2.	70 g	45 kg

	a	b	c
3.	32,000	7	1,800
4.	490	825,000	6,783
5.	0.0128	0.009	0.137
6.	5.268	0.025	0.0049

Page 102

	a	b
1.	200 mL	450 mL
2.	50 L	2.84 L

	a	b	c
3.	27,000	5,300	7,450
4.	825	2,000	39,600
5.	3.096	6	0.4125
6.	0.058	0.798	0.0192

Page 103

	a	b	c
1.	37 cm 1 mm	8 kg 125 g	11 L 775 mL
2.	1 kg 950 g	3 L 125 mL	22 m 95 cm
3.	28 km 125 m	35 kg 210 g	46 L 500 mL
4.	1 kg 275 g	3 L 840 mL	2 km 250 m

Page 105

1. decimeter
hectometer
decigram
hectogram

2. 9 different ways

3. 6 different ways

Page 106

	a	b	c
1.	13	210	78
2.	2,400	4,500	40
3.	42	21,000	28
4.	300 km	2.5 m	
5.	2g	3 L	
6.	$10\frac{1}{2}$	2	1.123
7.	0.0059	2	2.102
8.	2.5	$3\frac{1}{2}$	0.0215
9.	<	<	
10.	<	>	

11. 3 gal 1 qt.
1 cm 9 mm
1 L 4 mL
99 gal. 6 pt.

Page 107

12. 1 half dollar, 1 quarter
1 half dollar, 2 dimes,
1 nickel

13. black, silver
black, blue
black, clear

1 half dollar, 1 dime,
3 nickels
1 half dollar, 5 nickels

blue, silver
blue, clear
silver, clear

14. 9 outfits

Page 108

1. plane *PQR*
2. line *PQ* or line *RS*
3. line segment *PR* or line segment *RS*
4. ray *PQ* or ray *SR*
5. point *P* or point *R*
6. line *PQ* and line *RS*
7. line *RS* and line *SQ*
8. line *PR* and line *RS*

Page 109

	a	b	c	d
9.	line	ray	plane	line segment
10.	$\overline{AB}$ or $\overline{BA}$	B	$\overrightarrow{LM}$	$\overleftrightarrow{RS}$ or $\overleftrightarrow{SR}$

11. a: intersecting   b: parallel
c: perpendicular   d: intersecting

Page 110

	a	b	c	d
1.	∠*LMN* or ∠*NML*	∠*QRS* or ∠*SRQ*	∠*F*	∠*ABC* or ∠*CBA*
2.	obtuse	acute	right	straight

Page 111

	a	b
1.	not congruent	not congruent
2.	not congruent	congruent

Page 113

1. triangle

2. right angles or congruent angles

3. 22 feet

Page 114

	a	b	c
1.	16 units	14 units	10 units
2.	24 units	12 units	18 units
3.	16 units	20 units	22 units
4.	22 units	14 units	22 units

Page 115

	a	b	c
1.	54 in.	118 cm	9 m
2.	124 yd.	84 in.	$21\frac{1}{2}$ ft.
3.	45.8 m	200 mm	80 yd.
4.	334 cm	67.6 m	112 ft.

Page 116

	a	b	c
1.	12 sq. units	18 sq. units	18 sq. units
2.	8 sq. units	30 sq. units	10 sq. units
3.	28 sq. units	6 sq. units	24 sq. units
4.	15 sq. units	32 sq. units	20 sq. units

Page 117

	a	b	c
1.	270 sq. cm	3,276 sq. mm	$11\frac{1}{4}$ sq. ft.
2.	24.7 sq. m	76 sq. yd.	160 sq. ft.
3.	3,145 sq. in.	3.96 sq. m	75.25 sq. cm
4.	$10\frac{1}{8}$ sq. yd.	117 sq. m	28 sq. in.

Page 118

	a	b	c
1.	24 cubic units	60 cubic units	84 cubic units
2.	18 cubic units	90 cubic units	80 cubic units
3.	280 cubic units	200 cubic units	180 cubic units

Page 119

	a	b	c
1.	1,400 cu. ft.	6,000 cu. mm	15,232 cu. in.
2.	15.6 cu. cm	1,250 cu. in.	1,440 cu. ft.
3.	1,920 cu. yd.	281.6 cu. m	990 cu. yd.

Page 121

1. 480 cubic in.
2. $5,333\frac{1}{3}$ sq. yd.
3. 6,807.6 cubic cm
4. 222 in.
5. 1,110 m
6. 8 cans

Page 122

1. point *A* or point *B*
2. line *AC* or line *DF*
3. ∠*FBC*
4. ray *BE* or ray *DF*
5. line *DF* and line *AC*
6. line segment *AB* or line segment *BC*
7. ∠*ABE* and ∠*EBC*

	a	b	c
8.	18 units	15 sq. units	24 cu. units
9.	8.2 m	340 cm	$34\frac{2}{3}$ yd.
10.	168 sq. mm	$1,296\frac{1}{4}$ sq. in.	6.63 sq. cm
11.	432 cu. yd.	170 cu. m	225 cu. ft.

Page 123

12. rectangle

13. Anita and Tremont

14. $101\frac{3}{4}$ in.

15. area = 175 sq. cm
volume = 175 cu. cm